AutoCAD 2017 Tutorial
Second Level 3D Modeling

Randy H. Shih
Oregon Institute of Technology

SDC
Publications

SDC Publications
P.O. Box 1334
Mission, KS 66222
913-262-2664
www.SDCpublications.com
Publisher: Stephen Schroff

ISBN-13: 978-1-63057-038-5
ISBN-10: 1-63057-038-9

Printed and bound in the United States of America.

Preface

The primary goal of *AutoCAD® 2017 Tutorial Second Level 3D Modeling* is to introduce the aspects of **Computer Based Three Dimensional Modeling**. This text is intended to be used as a training guide for students and professionals. This text covers *AutoCAD 2017* and the chapters proceed in a pedagogical fashion to guide you from constructing 3D wireframe models, 3D surface models and 3D solid models to making multiview drawings. This text takes a hands-on, exercise-intensive approach to all the important 3D modeling techniques and concepts. This textbook contains a series of twelve tutorial style chapters designed to introduce CAD users to 3D modeling with **AutoCAD 2017**. This text is also helpful to AutoCAD users upgrading from a previous release of the software. The new improvements and enhancements of the software are incorporated into the tutorials. The 3D modeling techniques and concepts discussed in this text are also designed to serve as the foundation to the more advanced feature-based CAD/CAE packages such as AutoCAD® Architecture Desktop and Autodesk Inventor®. The basic premise of this book is that the more 3D designs you create using AutoCAD 2017, the better you learn the software. With this in mind, each tutorial introduces a new set of commands and concepts, building on previous chapters. This book does not attempt to cover all of AutoCAD 2017's features, only to provide an introduction to the software. It is intended to help you establish a good basis for exploring and growing in the exciting field of Computer Aided Engineering.

Acknowledgments

This book would not have been possible without a great deal of support. First, special thanks to two great teachers, Prof. George R. Schade of University of Nebraska-Lincoln and Mr. Denwu Lee, who taught me the fundamentals, the intrigue, and the sheer fun of Computer Aided Engineering.

The effort and support of the editorial and production staff of SDC Publications is gratefully acknowledged. I would especially like to thank Stephen Schroff for the support and helpful suggestions during this project.

I am grateful that the Department of Mechanical and Manufacturing Engineering Technology at Oregon Institute of Technology has provided me with an excellent environment in which to pursue my interests in teaching and research. I would especially like to thank Professor Brian Moravec and Emeritus Professor Charles Hermach for helpful comments and encouragement.

Finally, truly unbounded thanks are due to my wife Hsiu-Ling and our daughter Casandra for their understanding and encouragement throughout this project.

Randy H. Shih
Klamath Falls, Oregon
Spring, 2016

Table of Contents

Preface
Acknowledgments

Introduction
Getting Started

Introduction   Intro-2
Development of Computer Geometric Modeling   Intro-2
Why Use AutoCAD 2017   Intro-5
Getting Started with AutoCAD 2017   Intro-7
AutoCAD 2017 Screen Layout   Intro-8
Application Menu   Intro-9
Quick Access Toolbar   Intro-9
AutoCAD Menu Bar   Intro-9
Layout Tabs   Intro-9
Drawing Area   Intro-10
Graphics Cursor or Crosshairs   Intro-10
Command Prompt Area   Intro-10
Cursor Coordinates   Intro-10
Status Toolbar   Intro-10
Ribbon Tabs and Panels   Intro-11
Draw and Modify Toolbar Panels   Intro-11
Layers Control Toolbar Panel   Intro-11
Viewport/View/Display Controls   Intro-11
Mouse Buttons   Intro-12
[Esc] - Canceling commands   Intro-12
On-Line Help   Intro-13
Leaving AutoCAD 2017   Intro-14
Creating a CAD File Folder   Intro-14

Chapter 1
AutoCAD 2D Isometric Drawings

Introduction   1-2
The *Angle Support* Design   1-3
Starting Up AutoCAD 2017   1-4
AutoCAD ISOPLANE and ISODRAFT Commands   1-5
Layers Setup   1-6
Create the Base Box of the Design   1-7
Create the Design inside the Base Box   1-11
Create the Isocircle on the top face   1-14
Using the Editing Tools in an Isometric drawing   1-17
The Tube Anchor Design –Modeling Strategy   1-17

Start a New Drawing and Layers Setup   1-18
Create a Base Box of the Design   1-19
Locate the Centers for the Isocircles   1-22
Create the Isocircles   1-24
Using the Parametric tools to complete the drawing   1-31
Review Questions   1-36
Exercises   1-37

Chapter 2
User Coordinate System and the Z-Axis

Introduction   2-2
The Floor Plan Design   2-2
Starting Up AutoCAD 2017   2-3
3D Modeling WorkSpace   2-4
Drawing Units Setup   2-5
Drawing Area Setup   2-6
GRID and *SNAP* Intervals Setup   2-7
Create Polylines   2-9
Create an Offset Polyline   2-10
Create Interior Walls   2-11
Complete the Doorway Using the *TRIM* Command   2-14
User Coordinate System – It is an XY CRT, but an XYZ World   2-16
Viewing the 2D Design in 3D Space   2-17
Add the 3rd Dimension to the Floor Plan Design   2-18
View the Design Using the Hide Option   2-20
Add New Layers   2-21
Move Entities to a Different Layer   2-23
Reposition the UCS   2-23
Create the Roof   2-25
Rotating the UCS   2-27
Sketching on the Rotated UCS   2-28
View the Design Using the Hidden Option   2-29
Review Questions   2-30
Exercises   2-31

Chapter 3
3D Wireframe Modeling

Introduction   3-2
The Locator Design   3-3
Starting Up AutoCAD 2017   3-4
Activate the Startup Option   3-4
Create the Rectangular Base of the Design   3-6
Create a 3D Box   3-7
Object Snap Toolbar   3-10

Use the Snap Options to Locate the Top Corners   3-10
Use the Copy Option to Create Additional Edges   3-12
Use the Trim Command   3-14
Use the View Toolbar   3-16
Dynamic Rotation – Free Orbit   3-16
Use the *Offset* Command to Create Parallel Edges   3-17
Create a Circle above the UCS Sketch Plane   3-19
Complete the Wireframe Model   3-20
Review Questions   3-22
Exercises   3-23

Chapter 4
UCS, Viewports and Wireframe Modeling

Introduction   4-2
The V-Block Design   4-2
Starting Up AutoCAD 2017   4-3
3D Modeling Workspace   4-3
Layers Setup   4-4
Create the Rectangular Base of the Design   4-5
Create a Wireframe Box   4-6
Using the View and UCS Toolbars   4-7
Create Construction Lines in the Front View   4-8
Copy Objects in the Negative Z Direction   4-10
Create an Inclined Line at the Base of the Model   4-11
Create Object Lines   4-12
Multiple Viewports   4-14
Use the Mirror Command   4-15
Turn *OFF* the Construction Lines   4-17
Create a New UCS   4-18
Create a New Named View   4-20
Create the V-Cut Feature on the Inclined Plane   4-22
Extend the Cut and GRIP Editing   4-23
Review Questions   4-25
Exercises   4-26

Chapter 5
3D Surface Modeling

Introduction   5-2
Starting Up AutoCAD 2017   5-4
The UCS Toolbar and the Meshes Commands   5-5
Create a Mesh Surface Using the 2D Solid Command   5-5
Using the Visual Styles Toolbar   5-8
Create a Mesh Surface Using the 3D Face Command   5-10

The ViewCube   5-12
Create a Surface of Irregular Shape   5-14
Use the Invisible Edge Option   5-16
Repositioning with the Grip Editing Tools   5-17
The *Locator* Wireframe Model   5-18
Moving Objects to a Different Layer   5-18
Advanced Meshed Surface Modeling Commands   5-20
Use the Tabulated Surface Option   5-23
Use the Ruled Surface Option   5-24
Review Questions   5-27
Exercises   5-28

Chapter 6
Solid Modeling - Constructive Solid Geometry

Introduction   6-2
The Guide-Block Design   6-2
Constructive Solid Geometry Concept   6-3
Binary Tree   6-4
The Guide-Block CSG Binary Tree   6-5
Starting Up AutoCAD 2017   6-6
Layers Setup   6-7
Create the First 3D Object   6-7
Create the Second Solid Feature   6-9
Boolean Operation - *UNION*   6-10
Create the Second Cylinder Feature   6-11
Boolean Operation - *SUBTRACT*   6-12
Create another Solid Feature   6-13
Visual Styles Options   6-14
Create the Final Feature   6-15
Rotating the Rectangular Block   6-16
Reposition the Rectangular Block   6-17
The SteeringWheels   6-18
Review Questions   6-20
Exercises   6-21

Chapter 7
Regions, Extrude and Solid Modeling

Introduction   7-2
The *V-Block-Solid* Design   7-2
Starting Up AutoCAD 2017   7-3
Layers Setup   7-4
Setting Up a 2D Sketch   7-5
Defining the Front Edges of the Design   7-7
Create a Region   7-10

Extruding the Created Region   7-11
Create a 2D Sketch at the Base of the Model   7-13
Create a Copy of the 2D Sketch   7-14
Create the Cutter Solids   7-15
Boolean Operation - *Subtract*   7-16
Mass Properties of the Solid Model   7-17
Align the UCS to the Inclined Face   7-18
Create the *V-Cut*   7-19
Review Questions   7-22
Exercises   7-23

Chapter 8
Multiview Drawings from 3D Models

Introduction   8-2
The V-Block Design   8-2
Starting Up AutoCAD 2017   8-3
AutoCAD Paper Space   8-4
Delete the Displayed Viewport   8-5
Add Borders and Title Block in the Layout   8-6
Setting Up Viewports inside the Title Block   8-7
Setting Up the Standard Views   8-8
Determine the Necessary 2D Views   8-10
Establish an Auxiliary View in Model Mode   8-11
Add a Viewport for an Auxiliary View   8-13
Use the *DVIEW* Command   8-16
Adjust the Viewport Scale   8-17
Lock the Base View   8-18
Align the 2D Views   8-18
Create 2D Projected Entities - SOLPROF   8-21
Complete the 2D Drawing   8-23
Review Questions   8-25
Exercises   8-26

Chapter 9
Symmetrical Features in Designs

Introduction   9-2
A Revolved Design: Pulley   9-2
Modeling Strategy - A Revolved Design   9-3
Starting Up AutoCAD 2017   9-4
Layers Setup   9-5
Set Up a 2D Sketch for the Revolved Feature   9-6
Perform 2D Boolean Operations   9-8
Create the Revolved Feature   9-12
Mirrored Image of the Part   9-13

Combine Two Parts into One   9-14
Use the 3D Array command   9-15
Position and Perform the Cut   9-18
Review Questions   9-20
Exercises   9-21

Chapter 10
Advanced Modeling Tools & Techniques

Introduction   10-2
A Thin-Walled Design: OIL SINK   10-2
Modeling Strategy   10-3
Starting Up AutoCAD 2017   10-4
Layers Setup   10-5
The First Extruded Feature   10-6
Create an Offset Geometry from an Extracted Surface   10-8
Extrude with Draft Angle   10-10
Align the Parts   10-11
Create another Extracted Surface   10-12
Combining Parts – Boolean UNION   10-15
Create 3D Rounds and Fillets   10-16
Create a Shell Feature   10-18
Create a Rectangular Array Cut Feature   10-19
Create another Rectangular Array Cut Feature   10-21
Making a Design Change   10-23
Grip Editing Approach   10-23
Dynamic UCS Approach   10-24
Review Questions   10-27
Exercises   10-28

Chapter 11
Conceptual Design Tools & Techniques

Introduction   11-2
A Bird House Design   11-3
Starting Up AutoCAD 2017   11-4
Layers Setup   11-5
The Base Plate   11-6
Create the Compartments for the 1st Floor   11-7
Create a Solid Feature Using the Press/Pull Command   11-8
Using the Press/Pull Command as an Editing Tool   11-10
Create another Cut Feature   11-11
Adjust the Compartments   11-13
Add Additional Compartments   11-14
Create the Doors   11-15
Create the 2nd Floor   11-16

Reposition the 2nd Floor 11-18
Modeling the Roof Section with the Press/Pull Command 11-19
Use the Imprint Command 11-21
Review Questions 11-24
Exercises 11-25

Chapter 12
Introduction to Photorealistic Rendering

Introduction 12-2
Start Up AutoCAD 2017 and Retrieve the Pulley Design 12-3
Environment Setup 12-4
Use the Render Command 12-7
Available Lighting Simulation Modes in AutoCAD 12-8
Use the Materials Options 12-9
Activate the Sun & Sky Background Option 12-11
Add Additional Walls 12-14
Create a Point Light 12-17
Changing the Applied Materials 12-19
Create a Spotlight 12-20
Removing a Light 12-22
Create a Distant Light 12-23
Create New Materials 12-26
Save the Rendered Images 12-29
Conclusion 12-30
Review Questions 12-31
Exercises 12-32

Index

Notes:

Introduction
Getting Started

Learning Objectives

♦ **Development of Computer Aided Design**
♦ **Why use AutoCAD 2017?**
♦ **Getting started with AutoCAD 2017**
♦ **The AutoCAD Startup dialog box and Units setup**
♦ **AutoCAD 2017 screen layout**
♦ **Mouse buttons**

Introduction

Computer Aided Design (CAD) is the process of doing designs with the aid of computers. This includes the generation of computer models, analysis of design data, and the creation of the necessary drawings. **AutoCAD® 2017** is a computer-aided-design software developed by *Autodesk Inc*. The **AutoCAD® 2017** software is a tool that can be used for design and drafting activities. The two-dimensional and three-dimensional models created in **AutoCAD® 2017** can be transferred to other computer programs for further analysis and testing. The computer models can also be used in manufacturing equipment such as machining centers, lathes, mills, or rapid prototyping machines to manufacture the product.

The rapid changes in the field of **computer aided engineering** (CAE) have brought exciting advances in industry. Recent advances have made the long-sought goal of reducing design time, producing prototypes faster, and achieving higher product quality closer to a reality.

Development of Computer Geometric Modeling

Computer Aided Design is a relatively new technology and its rapid expansion in the last fifty years is truly amazing. Computer modeling technology advanced along with the development of computer hardware. The first generation CAD programs, developed in the 1950s, were mostly non-interactive; CAD users were required to create program codes to generate the desired two-dimensional (2D) geometric shapes. Initially, the development of CAD technology occurred mostly in academic research facilities. The Massachusetts Institute of Technology, Carnegie-Mellon University, and Cambridge University were the lead pioneers at that time. The interest in CAD technology spread quickly and several major industry companies, such as General Motors, Lockheed, McDonnell, IBM, and Ford Motor Co., participated in the development of interactive CAD programs in the 1960s. Usage of CAD systems was primarily in the automotive industry, aerospace industry, and government agencies that developed their own programs for their specific needs. The 1960s also marked the beginning of the development of finite element analysis methods for computer stress analysis and computer aided manufacturing for generating machine toolpaths.

The 1970s are generally viewed as the years of the most significant progress in the development of computer hardware, namely the invention and development of **microprocessors**. With the improvement in computing power, new types of 3D CAD programs that were user-friendly and interactive became reality. CAD technology quickly expanded from very simple **computer aided drafting** to very complex **computer aided design**. The use of 2D and 3D wireframe modelers was accepted as the leading edge technology that could increase productivity in industry. The developments of surface modeling and solid modeling technology were taking shape by the late 1970s, but the high cost of computer hardware and programming slowed the development of such technology. During this time period, the available CAD systems all required extremely expensive room-sized mainframe computers.

In the 1980s, improvements in computer hardware brought the power of mainframes to the desktop at less cost and with more accessibility to the general public. By the mid-1980s, CAD technology had become the main focus of a variety of manufacturing industries and was very competitive with traditional design/drafting methods. It was during this period of time that 3D solid modeling technology had major advancements, which boosted the usage of CAE technology in industry.

In the 1990s, CAD programs evolved into powerful design/manufacturing/management tools. CAD technology has come a long way, and during these years of development, modeling schemes progressed from two-dimensional (2D) wireframe to three-dimensional (3D) wireframe, to surface modeling, to solid modeling and, finally, to feature-based parametric solid modeling.

The first generation CAD packages were simply 2D **Computer Aided Drafting** programs, basically the electronic equivalents of the drafting board. For typical models, the use of this type of program would require that several views of the objects be created individually as they would be on the drafting board. The 3D designs remained in the designer's mind, not in the computer database. The mental translation of 3D objects to 2D views is required throughout the use of the packages. Although such systems have some advantages over traditional board drafting, they are still tedious and labor intensive. The need for the development of 3D modelers came quite naturally, given the limitations of the 2D drafting packages.

The development of the 3D wireframe modeler was a major leap in the area of computer modeling. The computer database in the 3D wireframe modeler contains the locations of all the points in space coordinates and it is sufficient to create just one model rather than multiple models. This single 3D model can then be viewed from any direction as needed. The 3D wireframe modelers require the least computer power and achieve reasonably good representation of 3D models. But because surface definition is not part of a wireframe model, all wireframe images have the inherent problem of ambiguity.

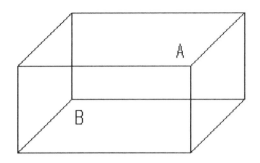

Wireframe Ambiguity: Which corner is in front, A or B?

A non-realizable object: Wireframe models contain no surface definitions.

Surface modeling is the logical development in computer geometry modeling to follow the 3D wireframe modeling scheme by organizing and grouping edges that define polygonal surfaces. Surface modeling describes the part's surfaces but not its interiors. Designers are still required to interactively examine surface models to ensure that the various surfaces on a model are contiguous throughout. Many of the concepts used in 3D wireframe and surface modelers are incorporated in the solid modeling scheme, but it is solid modeling that offers the most advantages as a design tool.

In the solid modeling presentation scheme, the solid definitions include nodes, edges, and surfaces, and it is a complete and unambiguous mathematical representation of a precisely enclosed and filled volume. Unlike the surface modeling method, solid modelers start with a solid or use topology rules to guarantee that all of the surfaces are stitched together properly. Two predominant methods for representing solid models are **constructive solid geometry** (CSG) representation and **boundary representation** (B-rep).

The CSG representation method can be defined as the combination of 3D solid primitives. What constitutes a "primitive" varies somewhat with the software but typically includes a rectangular prism, a cylinder, a cone, a wedge, and a sphere. Most solid modelers allow the user to define additional primitives, which can be very complex.

In the B-rep representation method, objects are represented in terms of their spatial boundaries. This method defines the points, edges, and surfaces of a volume, and/or issues commands that sweep or rotate a defined face into a third dimension to form a solid. The object is then made up of the unions of these surfaces that completely and precisely enclose a volume.

By the 1990s, a new paradigm called *concurrent engineering* had emerged. With concurrent engineering, designers, design engineers, analysts, manufacturing engineers, and management engineers all work closely right from the initial stages of the design. In this way, all aspects of the design can be evaluated and any potential problems can be identified right from the start and throughout the design process. Using the principles of concurrent engineering, a new type of computer modeling technique appeared. The technique is known as the *feature-based parametric modeling technique.* The key advantage of the *feature-based parametric modeling technique* is its capability to produce very flexible designs. Changes can be made easily and design alternatives can be evaluated with minimum effort. Various software packages offer different approaches to feature-based parametric modeling, yet the end result is a flexible design defined by its design variables and parametric features.

In this text, we will concentrate on creating designs using two-dimensional geometric construction techniques. The fundamental concepts and use of different **AutoCAD® 2017** commands are presented using step-by-step tutorials. We will begin with creating simple geometric entities and then move toward creating detailed working drawings and assembly drawings. The techniques presented in this text will also serve as the foundation for entering the world of three-dimensional solid modeling using packages such as **AutoCAD Mechanical Desktop, AutoCAD Architectural Desktop** and **Autodesk Inventor**.

Why Use AutoCAD® 2017?

AutoCAD® was first introduced to the public in late 1982 and was one of the first CAD software products that were available for personal computers. Since 1984, **AutoCAD®** has established a reputation for being the most widely used PC-based CAD software around the world. By 2010, it was estimated that there were over 6 million **AutoCAD®** users in more than 150 countries worldwide. **AutoCAD® 2017** is the thirty-first release, with many added features and enhancements, of the original **AutoCAD®** software produced by *Autodesk Inc.*

CAD provides us with a wide range of benefits; in most cases, the result of using CAD is increased accuracy and productivity. First of all, the computer offers much higher accuracy than the traditional methods of drafting and design. Traditionally, drafting and detailing are the most expensive cost element in a project and the biggest bottleneck.

With CAD systems, such as **AutoCAD® 2017,** the tedious drafting and detailing tasks are simplified through the use of many of the CAD geometric construction tools, such as *grids*, *snap*, *trim,* and *auto-dimensioning*. Dimensions and notes are always legible in CAD drawings, and in most cases, CAD systems can produce higher quality prints compared to traditional hand drawings.

CAD also offers much-needed flexibility in design and drafting. A CAD model generated on a computer consists of numeric data that describe the geometry of the object. This allows the designers and clients to see something tangible and to interpret the ramifications of the design. In many cases, it is also possible to simulate operating conditions on the computer and observe the results. Any kind of geometric shape stored in the database can be easily duplicated. For large and complex designs and drawings, particularly those involving similar shapes and repetitive operations, CAD approaches are very efficient and effective. Because computer designs and models can be altered easily, a multitude of design options can be examined and presented to a client before any construction or manufacturing actually takes place. Making changes to a CAD model is generally much faster than making changes to a traditional hand drawing. Only the affected components of the design need to be modified and the drawings can be plotted again. In addition, the greatest benefit is that, once the CAD model is created, it can be used over and over again. The CAD models can also be transferred into manufacturing equipment such as machining centers, lathes, mills, or rapid prototyping machines to manufacture the product directly.

CAD, however, does not replace every design activity. CAD may help, but it does not replace the designer's experience with geometry and graphical conventions and standards for the specific field. CAD is a powerful tool, but the use of this tool does not guarantee correct results; the designer is still responsible for using good design practice and applying good judgment. CAD will supplement these skills to ensure that the best design is obtained.

CAD designs and drawings are stored in binary form, usually as CAD files, to magnetic devices such as diskettes and hard disks. The information stored in CAD files usually requires much less physical space in comparison to traditional hand drawings. However, the information stored inside the computer is not indestructible. On the contrary, the electronic format of information is very fragile and sensitive to the environment. Heat or cold can damage the information stored on magnetic storage devices. A power failure while you are creating a design could wipe out the many hours you spent working in front of the computer monitor. It is a good habit to save your work periodically, just in case something might go wrong while you are working on your design. In general, one should save one's work onto a storage device at an interval of every 15 to 20 minutes. You should also save your work before you make any major modifications to the design. It is also a good habit to periodically make backup copies of your work and put them in a safe place.

Getting Started with AutoCAD 2017

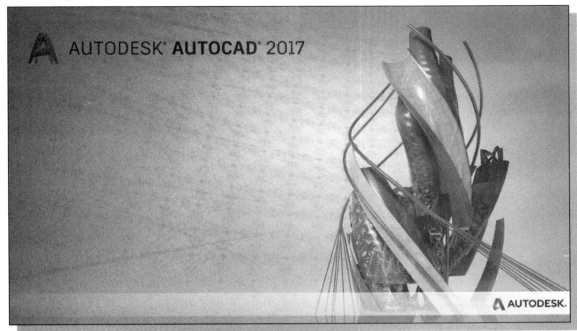

How to start **AutoCAD 2017** depends on the type of workstation and the particular software configuration you are using. With most *Windows* systems, you may select the **AutoCAD 2017** option on the *Start* menu or select the **AutoCAD 2017** icon on the *Desktop*. Consult with your instructor or technical support personnel if you have difficulty starting the software.

The program takes a while to load, so be patient. Eventually the **AutoCAD 2017** main *drawing screen* will appear on the screen. Click **Start Drawing** as shown in the below figure. The tutorials in this text are based on the assumption that you are using **AutoCAD 2017**'s default settings. If your system has been customized, some of the settings may not work with the step-by-step instructions in the tutorials. Contact your instructor and technical support to restore the default software configuration.

AutoCAD 2017 Screen Layout

The default **AutoCAD 2017** *drawing screen* contains the *pull-down* menus, the *Standard* toolbar, the *InfoCenter Help system,* the *scrollbars,* the *command prompt area*, the *Status Bar*, and the *Ribbon Tabs* and *Panels* that contain several *control panels* such as the *Draw and Modify* panel and the *Annotation* panel. You may resize the **AutoCAD 2017** drawing window by clicking and dragging at the edges of the window, or relocate the window by clicking and dragging at the window title area.

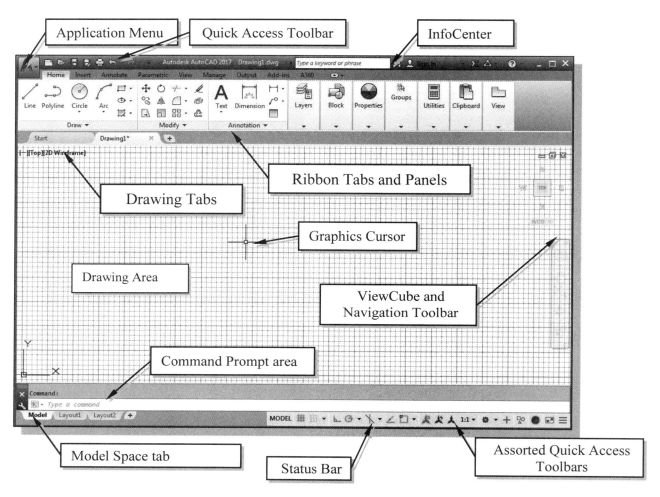

* Click on the down-arrow in the *Quick Access* bar and select **Show Menu Bar** to display the **AutoCAD** *Menu* bar. Note that the menu bar provides access to all of the AutoCAD commands.

Application Menu

The *Application Menu* at the top of the main window contains commonly used file operations.

Quick Access Toolbar

The *Quick Access* toolbar at the top of the *AutoCAD* window allows us quick access to frequently used commands, such as **Qnew, Open, Save** and also the **Undo** command. Note that we can customize the quick access toolbar by adding and removing sets of options or individual commands.

AutoCAD Menu Bar

The *Menu* bar is the pull-down menu where all operations of AutoCAD can be accessed.

Layout tabs

The Model/Layout tabs allow us to switch/create between different **model space** and **paper space**.

- **Drawing Area**
  The *Drawing Area* is the area where models and drawings are displayed.

- **Graphics Cursor or Crosshairs**

The *graphics cursor*, or *crosshairs*, shows the location of the pointing device in the Drawing Area. The coordinates of the cursor are displayed at the bottom of the screen layout. The cursor's appearance depends on the selected command or option.

- **Command Prompt Area**

The *Command Prompt Area* provides status information for an operation and it is also the area for data input. Note that the *Command Prompt* can be docked below the drawing area as shown.

- **Cursor Coordinates**

To switch on the **AutoCAD Coordinates Display**, use the *Customization option* at the bottom right corner.

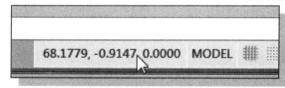

The bottom section of the screen layout displays the coordinate information of the cursor.

- **Status Toolbar**
  Next to the cursor coordinate display is the *Status* toolbar, showing the status of many commonly used display and construction options.

- **Ribbon Tabs and Panels**

  The top section of the screen layout contains customizable icon panels, which contain groups of buttons that allow us to pick commands quickly, without searching through a menu structure. These panels allow us to quickly access the commonly used commands available in AutoCAD.

- **Draw and Modify Toolbar Panels**

  The *Draw* and *Modify* toolbar panels are the two main panels for creating drawings; the toolbars contain icons for basic draw and modify commands.

Draw Toolbar

Modify Toolbar

- **Layers Control Toolbar Panel**

The *Layers Control* toolbar panel contains tools to help manipulate the properties of graphical objects.

- **Viewport/View/Display Controls**

The *Viewport/View/Display controls panel* is located at the upper left corner of the graphics area and it can be used to quickly access viewing related commands, such as Viewport and Display style.

Mouse Buttons

AutoCAD 2017 utilizes the mouse buttons extensively. In learning **AutoCAD 2017**'s interactive environment, it is important to understand the basic functions of the mouse buttons. It is highly recommended that you use a mouse or a tablet with **AutoCAD 2017** since the package uses the buttons for various functions.

- **Left mouse button**
  The **left-mouse-button** is used for most operations, such as selecting menus and icons or picking graphic entities. One click of the button is used to select icons, menus and form entries and to pick graphic items.

- **Right mouse button**
  The **right-mouse-button** is used to bring up additional available options. The software also utilizes the **right-mouse-button** the same as the **ENTER** key and is often used to accept the default setting to a prompt or to end a process.

- **Middle mouse button/wheel**
  The middle mouse button/wheel can be used to Pan (hold down the wheel button and drag the mouse) or Zoom (rotate the wheel) real time.

Allows quick Pan and Zoom.

Brings up additional available options. Also used to accept the default option of a command, or end a process.

Picks icons, menus, and graphic entities.

[Esc] – Canceling commands

The [**Esc**] key is used to cancel a command in **AutoCAD 2017**. The [**Esc**] key is located near the top-left corner of the keyboard. Sometimes, it may be necessary to press the [**Esc**] key twice to cancel a command; it depends on where we are in the command sequence. For some commands, the [**Esc**] key is used to exit the command.

Online Help

❖ Several types of online help are available at any time during an **AutoCAD 2017** session. The **AutoCAD 2017** software provides many online help options:

- **Autodesk Exchange**:
  Autodesk Exchange is a central portal in AutoCAD 2017; AutoCAD Exchange provides a user interface for Help, learning aids, tips and tricks, videos, and downloadable apps. By default, *Autodesk Exchange* is displayed at **startup**. This allows access to a dynamic selection of tools from the *Autodesk community*; note that an internet connection is required to use this option.

- To use *Autodesk Exchange*, simply type in a question in the *input box* to search through the Autodesk's *Help* system as shown.

- A list of the search results appears in the *Autodesk Help* window, and we can also determine the level and type of searches of the associated information.

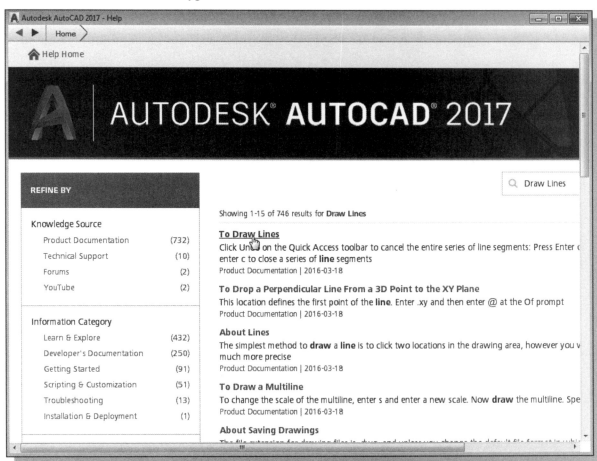

Leaving AutoCAD 2017

➢ To leave **AutoCAD 2017**, use the left-mouse-button and click the **Application Menu** button at the top left corner of the **AutoCAD 2017** screen window, then choose **Exit AutoCAD** from the pull-down menu or type **QUIT** in the command prompt area.

   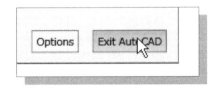

Creating a CAD File Folder

❖ It is a good practice to create a separate folder to store your CAD files. You should not save your CAD files in the same folder where the **AutoCAD 2017** application is located. It is much easier to organize and back up your project files if they are in a separate folder. Making folders within this folder for different types of projects will help you organize your CAD files even further.

➢ To create a new folder in the *Microsoft Windows* environment:

1. On the *desktop* or under the *My Documents* folder, in which you want to create a new folder,

2. Right-click once to bring up the option menu, then select New➔ Folder.

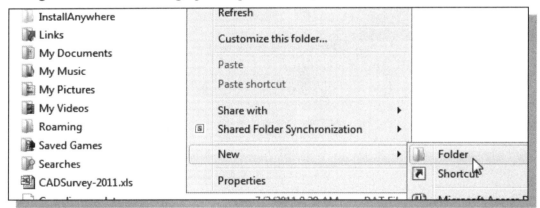

3. Type a name for the new folder, and then press **ENTER**.

Chapter 1
AutoCAD 2D Isometric Drawings

Learning Objectives

- ◆ **Understand the Axonometric projections**
- ◆ **Use the AutoCAD 2D Isometric Drawing tools**
- ◆ **Understand and Use the AutoCAD ISOPLANE and ISODRAFT commands**
- ◆ **Create the AutoCAD ISOCIRCLES**
- ◆ **Use the Object Snap options**
- ◆ **Control Objects with the Parametric Geometry Constraint tools**

Introduction

Although AutoCAD has full 3D solid modeling capabilities, it makes sense to use isometric drawing when all that is needed is some simple isometric views for design concepts and /or presentations. AutoCAD's 2D Isometric drawing is a simple 2D drawing to represent a 3D object. The Isometric projection is a type of **axonometric projection**; the word *axonometric* means "to measure along axes." There are three types of axonometric projections: isometric projection, dimetric projection, and trimetric projection. Typically in an axonometric drawing, one axis is drawn vertically.

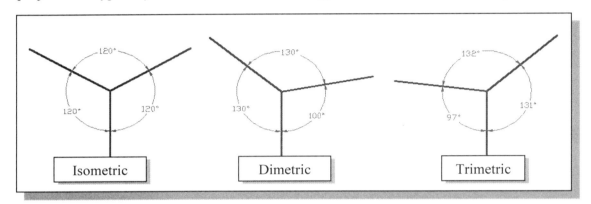

In **isometric projections**, the direction of viewing is such that the three axes of space appear equally foreshortened, and therefore the angles between the three axes are equal. While in **dimetric projections** and **trimetric projections** the directions of viewing are such that not all three axes of space appear equally foreshortened.

Isometric drawing is perhaps the most widely used for pictorials in engineering graphics, mainly because isometric views are the most convenient to draw. To create an isometric drawing, the visible portions of the individual 2D-views are constructed on the corresponding sides of the box. Adjustments of the locations of surfaces are then made, by moving the edges, to complete the isometric view.

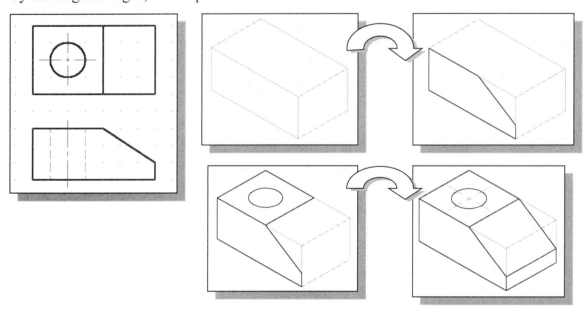

In an isometric drawing, cylindrical or circular shapes appear as ellipses. It can be confusing drawing the ellipses in an isometric view; one simple rule to remember is the **major axis** of the ellipse is always **perpendicular** to the **center axis** of the cylinder as shown in the figures below.

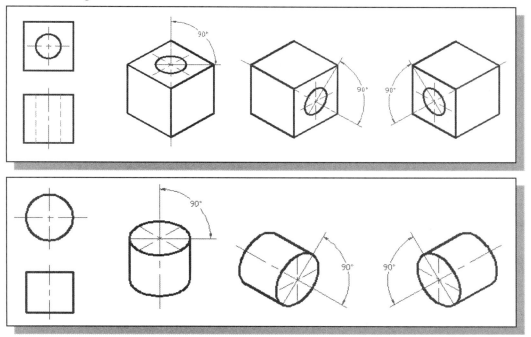

The general procedure to constructing AutoCAD 2D isometric drawing is illustrated in the following sections. Note that this is a fairly simple and effective way of representing a three dimensional object in two dimensional space.

The *Angle Support* Design

Starting Up AutoCAD 2017

1. Select the **AutoCAD 2017** option on the *Program* menu or select the **AutoCAD 2017** icon on the *Desktop*. Once the program is loaded into memory, the **AutoCAD 2017** drawing screen will appear on the screen.

Note that AutoCAD automatically assigns generic name, *Drawing X*, as new drawings are created. In our example, AutoCAD opened the graphics window using the default system units and assigned the drawing name *Drawing1*.

2. If necessary, click on the down-arrow in the *Quick Access Bar* and select **Show Menu Bar** to display the **AutoCAD** *Menu Bar*. The *Menu Bar* provides access to all AutoCAD commands.

AutoCAD ISOPLANE and ISODRAFT Commands

AutoCAD uses the ISOPLANE and ISODRAFT commands to control the alignment of the cursor to the three isometric axes. The following settings can be used when drawing 2D isometric representations of 3D models:

- Ortho directions
- Snap orientation
- Grid orientation and style
- Polar tracking angles
- Orientation of isometric circles

The isometric plane affects the cursor movement only when the snap style is set to *Isometric* in the *Drafting Settings* dialog box. If the snap option is set to Isometric, Ortho mode uses the appropriate axis paired to 30, 90, and/or 150 degrees.

Left Plane

 The cursor is aligned to the left-facing plane of the isometric axes.

Top Plane

 The cursor is aligned to the top-facing plane of the isometric axes.

Right Plane

 The cursor is aligned to the right-facing plane of the isometric axes.

➢ The three isometric planes can be selected by toggling the [**F5**] or [**Ctrl+E**] keys or use the **ISODRAFT** command.

The ISODRAFT command can be accessed through the icon in the *Status Bar* area. The primary advantage of ISODRAFT is that when it is toggled on, all the related settings are automatically set as well, so the cursor will be aligned to the isometric axes of the active *Isoplane*.

Layers Setup

1. Click **Layer Properties Manager** in the *Layers* toolbar.

❖ In AutoCAD, we always construct entities on a layer. It may be the default layer or a layer that we create. Each layer has associated properties such as the visibility setting, color, linetype, lineweight, and plot style.

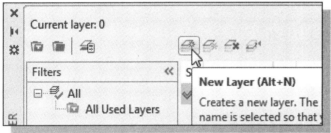

2. Click on the **New Layer** button. Notice a layer is automatically added to the list of layers.

3. Create **two new layers** with the following settings:

Layer	Color	Linetype	Lineweight
Construction	Grey	Continuous	Default
Object	Cyan	Continuous	0.30mm

4. Highlight the layer *Construction* in the list of layers.

5. Click on the **Current** icon to set layer *Construction* as the *Current Layer*.

6. Click on the **Close** button to accept the settings and exit the *Layer Properties Manager* dialog box.

Create the Base Box of the Design

- We will first use construction geometry to define the outer edges of the design.

1. In the *Layer Control* box, confirm that layer *Construction* is set as the *Current Layer*.

2. Click on the *Customization* icon, switch **on** the **Isometric Drafting** option as shown.

 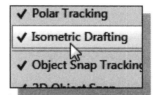

3. In the *Status Bar* area, reset the option buttons so that only the *GRID DISPLAY, Dynamic Input, Object Snap Tracking* and *Object Snap* options are switched **ON**.

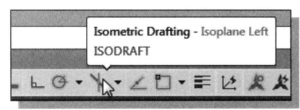

4. In the *Status Bar* area, click on the **Isodraft** icon to switch **on** the *Isoplane* option. Note the default isoplane is set to the *Left plane*.

5. Inside the graphics area, notice the cursor is set to align to the *Left Isoplane*. The *Grid Points* are also aligned to the isoplane.

6. Hit the [**F5**] key or [**Ctrl+E**] once and notice the isoplane is now set to the *Top plane* as shown.

7. Hit the [**F5**] key or [**Ctrl+E**] twice and notice the isoplane is now set back to the *Left plane* as shown.

➤ Note that we can also click on the arrow next to the *Isodraft* icon to show and/or set the active *isoplane*.

8. In the *Status Bar* area, click on the **Snap Mode** icon to switch **on** the *Snap to Grid* option.

9. Activate the **Line** command in the *Draw* toolbar. Note that since the *Snap* mode is switched on, the cursor is aligned to the grid points in the directions of the left isoplane.

10. Place the first endpoint of the line near the center of the graphics area.

11. Move the cursor downward, and enter **1.5** as the distance to the second end point of the line sequence.

12. Move the cursor toward the left side, and align the cursor in the 150 degrees direction. Enter **3.5** as the distance to the third end point of the line sequence.

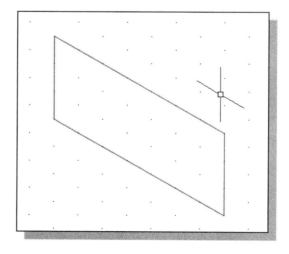

13. Repeat the above steps and create the front face of the isometric box for the *Angle Support design*.

14. Hit the [**Esc**] key once to end the line sequence.

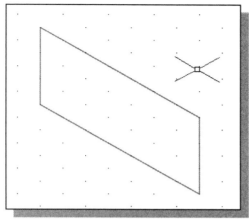

15. Hit the [**F5**] key or [**Ctrl+E**] once and notice the isoplane is now set back to the *Top plane* as shown.

16. Activate the **Line** command in the *Draw* toolbar.

17. Snap to the **top left corner** of the polygon we just created.

18. Move the cursor toward the right side, and align the cursor in the 30 degrees direction. Enter **2.0** as the distance to the second end point of the line sequence.

19. Move the cursor toward the right side, and align the cursor in the -30 degrees direction. Enter **3.5** as the distance to the third end point of the line sequence.

20. Snap to the **top right corner** of the front face of the isometric box to form the top face of the isometric box.

21. Hit the [**Esc**] key once to end the line sequence.

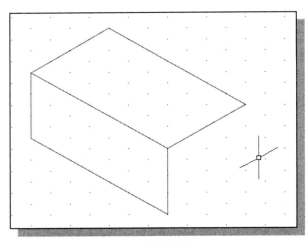

22. Hit the [**F5**] key or [**Ctrl+E**] once and notice the isoplane is now set to the *Right plane* as shown.

23. Activate the **Line** command in the *Draw* toolbar.

24. Move the cursor downward, and enter **1.5** as the distance to the second end point of the line sequence.

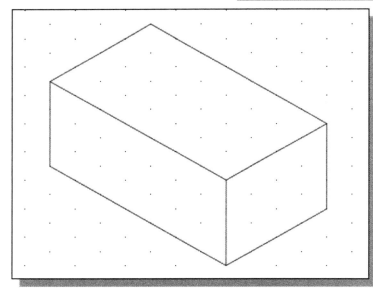

25. Snap to the **lower right corner** of the front face of the isometric box to form the right face of the isometric box.

• We will use the isometric box to help creating the *Angle Support design.* Note that the entire process is done in two dimensional space to represent a 3D design.

Create the Design inside the Base Box

- We will now create the design using the base isometric box.

1. In the *Layer Control* box, set the layer *Object* as the *Current Layer*.

2. In the *Menu Bar* select **[Tools]** → **[Toolbars]** → **[AutoCAD]** → **[Object Snap]**.

3. Activate the **Line** command in the *Draw* toolbar.

4. In the *command prompt* area, the message "*_line Specify first point:*" is displayed. Select **Snap From** in the *Object Snap* toolbar.

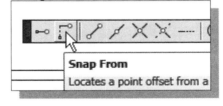

5. Select the **top left corner** of the base box as the reference point as shown.

6. Move the cursor along the top edge of the front face and select the location at 2 units at 330 degrees (**2.0<330**) as shown.

7. Snap to the **top left corner** of the base box as shown.

8. Follow along the front face of the base box and click on the three corners to create the three line segments as shown.

9. Move the cursor upward, and enter **0.5** as the distance to the next end point of the line sequence.

10. Right-click once to bring up the *option* list, and select **Close** to complete the front face of the design as shown.

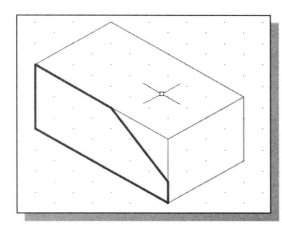

11. Hit the [**F5**] key or [**Ctrl+E**] once and notice the isoplane is now set to the *Top plane* as shown.

12. In the Status Bar area, switch on Object Snap tracking as shown.

13. Activate the **Line** command in the *Draw* toolbar.

14. Snap to the **top left corner** of the base box and create the two line segment as shown. (Hint: Use the *AutoSnap* option to locate the corresponding corner.)

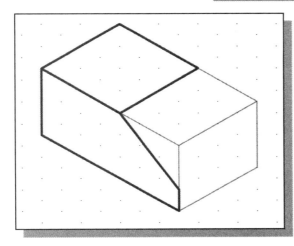

15. Complete the outlines of the top face of the design as shown.

16. Hit the [**Esc**] key once to end the line sequence.

Create the Isocircle on the top face

➢ In an isometric drawing, cylindrical or circular shapes appear as ellipses. In AutoCAD, the current aligned isometric plane also determines the orientation of isometric circles created with the **Isocircle** option of the *ELLIPSE* command.

1. In the *Layer Control* box, set the layer *Construction* as the *Current Layer*.

2. Activate the **Line** command in the *Draw* toolbar.

3. In the *command prompt* area, the message "*_line Specify first point:*" is displayed. Select **Midpoint** in the *Object Snap* toolbar.

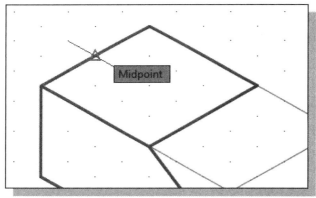

4. Select the midpoint of the top left edge of the top face of the design as shown.

5. Repeat the above step and create the two construction lines as shown. Note the intersection of the two lines identifies the center point of the circle.

6. In the *Layer Control* box, set the layer *Object* as the *Current Layer*.

7. In the *Draw* toolbar, activate the **Axis, End Ellipse** command.

➤ In AutoCAD, the isometric circles are created with the **Isocircle** option of the *ELLIPSE* command (available with *Axis, End* or *Elliptical Arc* options).

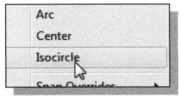

8. Right-click once to bring up the *option* list, and select **Isocircle** to create an isometric circle in an isometric view.

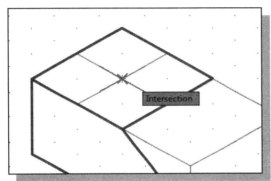

9. Select the intersection of the two construction lines we created in the previous section.

10. Enter **0.5** as the radius of the isocircle.

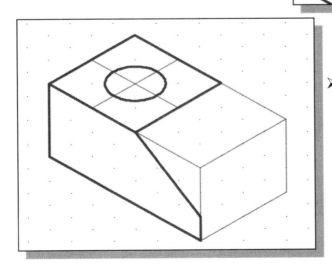

➤ In AutoCAD, the current aligned isometric top plane also determines the orientation of isometric circles created with the **Isocircle** option of the *ELLIPSE* command.

11. Hit the [**F5**] key or [**Ctrl+E**] once and notice the isoplane is now set to the *right plane* as shown.

12. In the *Draw* toolbar, activate the **Line** command as shown.

13. Snap to the **lower right corner** of the front face of the base box and create the two line segment as shown. (Hint: Use the *AutoSnap* option to locate the corresponding corner.)

14. On your own, complete the Isometric drawing as shown.

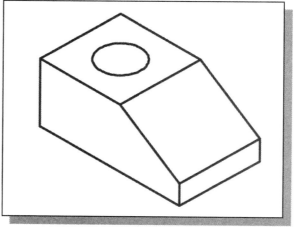

Using the Editing Tools in an Isometric drawing

➢ In AutoCAD, the commonly used editing tools, such as **Move, Copy, Trim, Extend**, and **Erase**, can also be used to aid the construction of an isometric drawing. In the following section, the *Tube Anchor* design will be created using some of the AutoCAD editing tools.

The Tube Anchor Design –Modeling Strategy

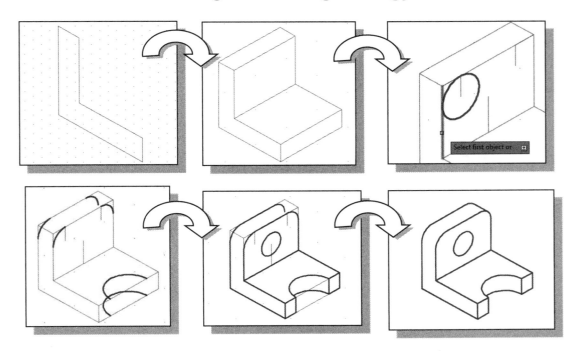

Start a New Drawing and Layers Setup

1. In the *Quick Access toolbar,* select **[New]**.

2. On your own, start a new English Units drawing.

3. Click **Layer Properties Manager** in the *Layers* toolbar.

❖   In AutoCAD, we always construct entities on a layer. It may be the default layer or a layer that we create. Each layer has associated properties such as the visibility setting, color, linetype, lineweight, and plot style.

4. Click on the **New Layer** button. Notice a layer is automatically added to the list of layers.

5. Create **two new layers** with the following settings:

Layer	Color	Linetype	Lineweight
Construction	Grey	Continuous	Default
Object	Cyan	Continuous	0.30mm

6. Highlight the layer *Construction* in the list of layers.

7. Click on the **Current** icon to set layer *Construction* as the *Current Layer*.

8. Click on the **Close** button to accept the settings and exit the *Layer Properties Manager* dialog box.

Create a Base Box of the Design

- We will first use construction geometry to define the outer edges of the design.

1. In the *Status Bar* area, reset the option buttons so that only the *Grid Display, Dynamic Input, Ortho, Isodraft, Object Snap Tracking, Object Snap* and *LineWeight* options are switched **ON**.

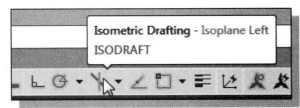

2. In the *Status Bar* area, set the *Isoplane* option to the *Left plane* as shown.

3. Activate the **Line** command in the *Draw* toolbar. Note that since the **Ortho** mode is switched on, the cursor is now aligned to the axes directions of the left isoplane.

4. Place the first endpoint of the line near the lower center of the graphics area.

5. Move the cursor downward, and enter **1.25** as the distance to the second end point of the line sequence.

6. Move the cursor toward the left side, and align the cursor in the 150 degrees direction. Enter **5.0** as the distance to the third end point of the line sequence.

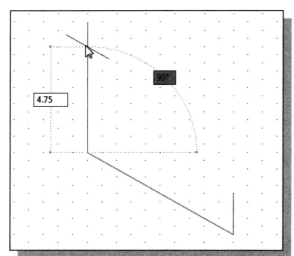

7. Move the cursor upward, and enter **4.75** as the distance to the next end point of the line sequence.

8. Move the cursor toward the left side, and align the cursor in the -30 degrees direction. Enter **1.25** as the distance to the next end point of the line sequence.

9. Move the cursor downward, and enter **3.5** as the distance to the second end point of the line sequence.

10. Right-click once to bring up the *option* list, and select **Close** to complete the front face of the design as shown.

11. Hit the [**F5**] key or [**Ctrl+E**] once and notice the isoplane is now set to the *Top plane* as shown.

12. In the modify toolbar, activate the **Copy** command as shown.

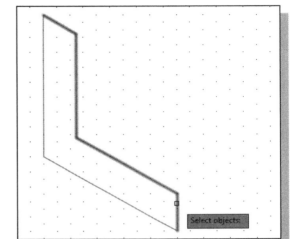

13. Select the four line segments as shown.

14. Right-click once to accept the selection and proceed with the **Copy** command.

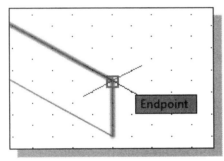

15. Select **one of the corners** as the copy reference point.

16. Move the cursor toward the right side and enter **5** as the distance to place the copy.

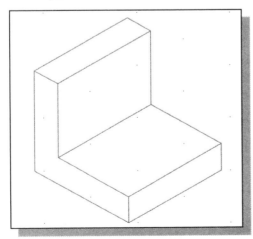

17. On your own, create additional lines to connect the corners of the front and back sides as shown.

Locate the Centers for the Isocircles

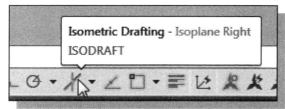

1. Hit the [**F5**] key or [**Ctrl+E**] once and notice the isoplane is now set to the *Right plane* as shown.

2. Activate the **Line** command in the *Draw* toolbar.

• We will first locate the center of the diameter 1.75 center circle of the design.

3. Activate the **Snap to Midpoint** option as shown.

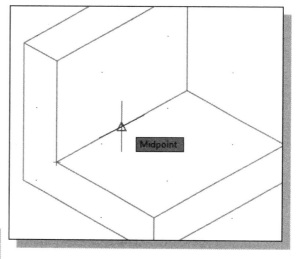

4. Select the bottom edge of the vertical section of the design as shown.

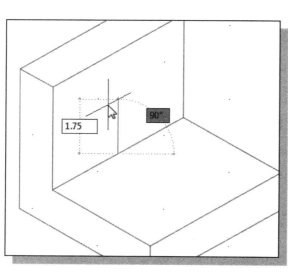

5. Move the cursor upward, and enter **1.75** as the distance to the center point of the diameter 1.75 circle.

6. Hit the [**Esc**] key once to end the line command.

- We will also need to locate the center locations for the two rounded corners of the vertical section of the design.

7. Activate the **Line** command in the *Draw* toolbar.

8. Snap to the upper left corner of the vertical section as shown.

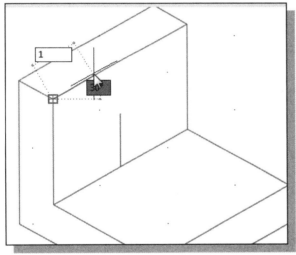

9. Move the cursor along the top edge, and enter **1.0** as the distance as shown.

10. Move the cursor downward, and enter **1.0** as the distance to locate the center point for the rounded corner as shown.

11. On your own, create two line segments to locate the center location of the rounded corner on the other side.

Create the Isocircles

1. In the *Layer Control* box, set the layer *Object* as the *Current Layer*.

2. In the *Draw* toolbar, activate the **Axis, End Ellipse** command.

3. In the command prompt area, click Isocircle as shown.

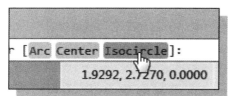

4. Snap to the bottom endpoint of the left line segment to place the center of the isocircle.

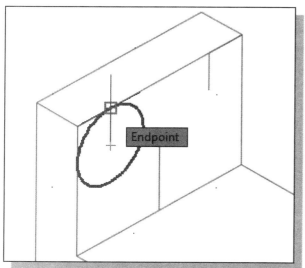

5. Snap to the top endpoint of the left line segment to create the isocircle representing the rounded corner.

- Note that the *Fillet* command **does not** create the correct rounded corner in AutoCAD *Isometric views*; we will confirm this is the case.

6. In the *Modify* toolbar, activate the **Fillet** command.

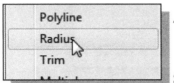

7. Right-mouse-click once to bring up the option list and select the **Radius** option.

8. Enter **1.0** as the radius of the fillet.

9. Select the left vertical edge as the first object as shown.

10. Select the top edge as the second object as shown.

11. On your own, create a circle on top of the arc created with the fillet command to confirm the circle is aligned to the screen, not the isometric axes.

12. In the *Draw* toolbar, activate the **Elliptical Arc** command as shown.

13. In the command prompt area, click Isocircle as shown.

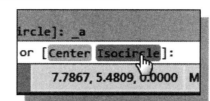

14. Snap to the bottom endpoint of the right line segment to place the center of the isocircle.

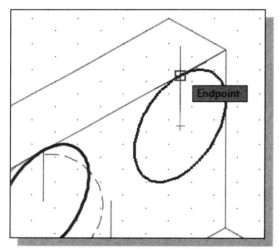

15. Snap to the top endpoint of the right line segment to accept the distance as radius.

16. Select the Endpoint angle 90 degree location as the start angle of the arc.

17. Snap to the top endpoint of the right line segment to accept the location as the end angle of the arc.

18. In the *Modify* toolbar, activate the **Trim** command as shown.

19. Select the top and the left edges as the trimming boundary as shown.

20. Click once with the right-mouse-button to accept the selection.

21. Click on the lower side of the isocircle to remove the lower portion as shown.

22. On your own, exit the trim command with the option list as shown.

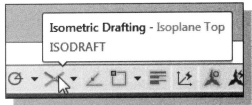

23. Hit the [**F5**] key or [**Ctrl+E**] twice and notice the isoplane is now set to the *top plane* as shown.

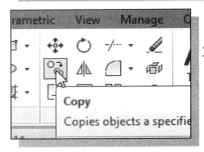

24. In the modify toolbar, activate the **Copy** command.

25. Select the two elliptical arcs as shown.

26. Right-mouse-click once to accept the selection and proceed with the **Copy** command.

27. Select the **Front left corner** as the copy reference point.

28. Select the **back left corner** to place the two copies of arcs.

29. Hit the [**Esc**] key once to end the copy command.

30. In the status bar area, turn off the Ortho mode as shown.

31. In the *Draw* toolbar, activate the **Axis, End Ellipse** command.

32. In the command prompt area, click Isocircle as shown.

33. Activate the **Snap to Midpoint** option as shown.

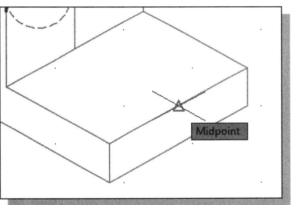

34. Snap to the midpoint of the top edge of the horizontal section of the design to place the center of the isocircle.

35. Enter **1.5** as the radius and create the isocircle.

36. On your own, use the trim and copy commands to create a copy of the elliptical arc to the bottom surface as shown.

37. Activate the **Line** command in the *Draw* toolbar.

38. On your own, create the outline of the design by creating line segments connecting to the arcs as shown in the below figure.

• Note that we need to identify the tangent edge for the top corner of the design.

Using the Parametric tools to complete the drawing

1. In the *Status Bar* area, turn off the *Isodraft*, *Object Snap Tracking* and *Object Snap* options as shown.

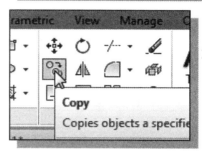

2. In the *modify toolbar*, activate the **Copy** command.

3. Select the **right edge** on the top face as shown.

4. Right-mouse-click once to accept the selection and proceed with the **Copy** command.

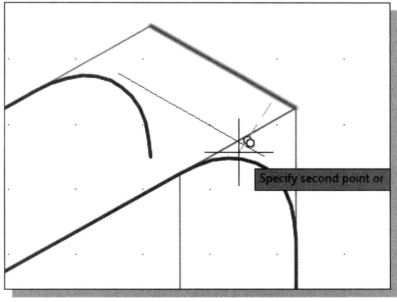

5. Select near the **right corner** as the copy reference point.

6. Place the line next to the two elliptical arcs; we will intentionally leave a gap.

7. Hit the [**Esc**] key once to exit the copy command.

8. In the *Ribbon* toolbar, switch to the **Parametric toolbar** as shown.

9. In the *Geometric* toolbar, activate the **Fix** constraint by clicking on the **Lock** icon as shown.

10. Right-mouse-click once to bring up the *option* list, and select **Object** to apply the constraint to an object.

11. Select the arc on the left to apply the fix constraint.

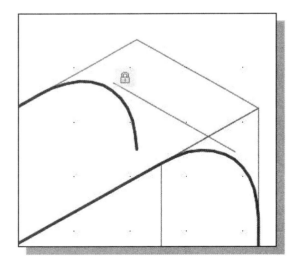

•   The lock icon next to the arc indicates the object is fixed to its current location.

12. In the *Geometric* toolbar, activate the **Tangent** constraint by clicking on the icon as shown.

13. Select the inclined line as the first object to apply the tangent constraint.

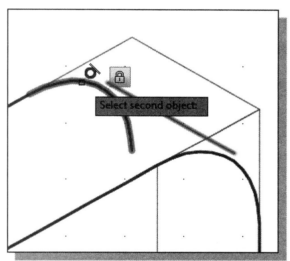

14. Select the fixed arc as the second object to apply the tangent constraint.

15. Click on the **Coincident** constraint as shown.

16. Click on the left end point of the line as shown.

17. Right-mouse-click once to bring up the *option* list, and select **Object** to apply the constraint to an object.

18. Select the fixed arc as the object to apply the constraint.

- Note the line is moved in place as the constraints are applied.

19. Click on the **Hide All** icon to remove all the constraints on the screen.

20. Click on the **Home** tab to switch back to the default 2D drawing toolbars.

21. On your own, move the tangent line to the **Object layer**.

22. In the *Layer control* box, turn off the Construction layer as shown.

23. In the *Modify* toolbar, activate the **Trim** command as shown.

24. Select the inclined line as the trimming boundary.

25. Click once with the right-mouse-button to accept the selection.

26. Trim the lower portion of the arc and complete the isometric drawing as shown.

Review Questions:

1. What is the difference between *Isometric* and *Trimetric projections*?

2. In an isometric drawing, how do we determine the directions of the ellipses in representing cylindrical or circular shapes?

3. Describe some of the advantages and disadvantages of using the AutoCAD **2D Isometric** drawings over creating 3D models.

4. Can the Fillet command be used to create accurate rounded corners in AutoCAD 2D isometric drawings?

5. What are the axes directions when the AutoCAD **Isoplane** is set to **Left plane**?

6. Identify the following commands:

(a)

(b)

(c)

(d)

Exercises:

1. Dimensions are in inches. Thickness: Base 0.5 & Boss height 0.25
   The two diameter 1.00 holes are through holes.

2. Dimensions are in inches.

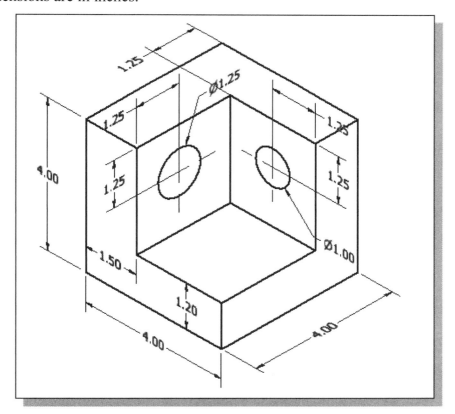

3. Dimensions are in inches.

4. Dimensions are in inches.

Chapter 2
User Coordinate Systems and the Z-Axis

Learning Objectives

- ♦ **Use the Drawing Units and Drawing Limits Commands**
- ♦ **Understand and Use the THICKNESS Option**
- ♦ **Understand the AutoCAD UCS**
- ♦ **Be able to Switch to Predefined Views**
- ♦ **Pre-selection of Objects**
- ♦ **Control Object Properties**
- ♦ **View with the Visual Styles Option**

Introduction

Creating three-dimensional models on a CAD system provides us a means to check the integrity of a design. Creating realistic three-dimensional models helps us visualize our final design much more clearly than we can with 2D representations of the design. Several different approaches are available in AutoCAD that allow us to quickly create 3D models. The simplest approach is to use the *Thickness* variable to perform an extrusion in the third dimension of 2D geometries. In AutoCAD, the *Thickness* variable can make certain 2D objects look like 3D objects. It is important to realize that this approach is somewhat limited and that the objects created are not true solids. This approach allows us to start considering the complexity involved in creating 3D models.

In this chapter, we will explore the virtual 3D environment in AutoCAD. Understanding how to maneuver in the virtual 3D environment and the use of a *User Coordinate System* (UCS) are the foundations and perhaps the most difficult parts of 3D modeling. We will also examine the basic viewing and rendering options that are available in AutoCAD. Specifically, we will use the **Hide** options to create hidden-line-removed images. The hidden-line-removed image makes it easier to visualize the model because the back faces are not displayed.

In this chapter, we will begin with the construction of a 2D floor plan design. This tutorial will also serve as a review of some of the 2D CAD construction techniques. The main goal of this chapter is to provide you with a basic understanding of the 3D environment of AutoCAD.

The *Floor Plan* Design

Starting Up AutoCAD 2017

1. Select the **AutoCAD 2017** option on the *Program* menu or select the **AutoCAD 2017** icon on the *Desktop*. Once the program is loaded into memory, the **AutoCAD 2017** drawing screen will appear on the screen.

Note that AutoCAD automatically assigns a generic name, *Drawing X*, as new drawings are created. In our example, AutoCAD opened the graphics window using the default system units and assigned the drawing name *Drawing1*.

2. If necessary, click on the down-arrow in the *Quick Access Bar* and select **Show Menu Bar** to display the **AutoCAD** *Menu Bar*. The *Menu Bar* provides access to all AutoCAD commands.

3D Basic Modeling WorkSpace

➢ Turn on the **Workspace** option in the **Quick Access Toolbar** as shown.

• *Workspaces* are sets of menus, toolbars, palettes, and control panels that are grouped and organized so that the user can work in a custom, task-oriented drawing environment. Workspaces control the display of menus, toolbars, and palettes in the drawing area. By default, AutoCAD is set to the *Drafting and annotation Workspace*, which is typically used for **2D Drafting**.

AutoCAD 2017 provides three pre-defined task-based workspaces:
• Drafting & Annotation
• 3D Basics
• 3D Modeling

For example, the *Drafting & Annotation* workspace displays most of the toolbars and menus commonly used for 2D drafting tasks. The *3D Basics* workspace contains only the very basic 3D-related toolbars, where the *3D Modeling* workspace contains more complete 3D surfacing and solid-related toolbars, menus, and palettes.

When we use a workspace, we change the display of the AutoCAD drawing area. It is also important to note that we can still create 3D models using the *Drafting & Annotation* workspace. All of the AutoCAD commands are available regardless which workspace we use. Using the workspaces is one of the many options available in AutoCAD 2017 that can help simplify our drafting/modeling tasks.

1. Click on the workspaces list in the *Workspace* toolbar and choose to use the **3D Basics** workspace as shown.

➢ Notice the different toolbars available in the *Ribbon* toolbar area as shown.

Drawing Units Setup

➢ Every object we construct in a CAD system is measured in **units**. We should determine the value of the units within the CAD system before creating the first geometric entities.

1. On your own, turn **on** the display of the **Menu Bar**.

2. In the *Menu Bar* area, select:

   [Format] → [Units]

3. In the *Drawing Units* dialog box, set the *Length Type* to **Architectural**. This will set the measurement to the default **Architectural units, feet and inches**.

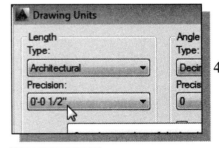

4. Set the *Precision* to **half-an-inch** as shown in the figure.

5. Click **OK** to exit the *Drawing Units* dialog box.

Drawing Area Setup

❖ Next, we will set up the **Drawing Limits**; setting the Drawing Limits controls the extents of the display of the *grid*. It also serves as a visual reference that marks the working area. It can also be used to prevent construction outside the grid limits and also as a plot option that defines an area to be plotted/printed. Note that this setting does not limit the region for geometry construction.

1. In the *Menu Bar* area, select:

   [Format] → [Drawing Limits]

2. In the command prompt area, near the bottom of the AutoCAD drawing screen, the message "*Reset Model Space Limits: Specify lower left corner or [On/Off] <0'-0", 0'-0">:*" is displayed. Press the **ENTER** key once to accept the default coordinates **<0'-0", 0'-0">**.

   ```
   Command: '_limits
   Reset Model space limits:
   ⊞ ▾ LIMITS Specify lower left corner or [ON OFF] <0'-0",0'-0">:
   Model   Layout1   Layout2   ✱                              1'-2", 0'-4 1
   ```

3. In the command prompt area, the message "*Specify upper right corner <1'-0", 0'-9">:*" is displayed. Enter **60', 40'** to change the upper right coordinates to **<60', 40'>**.

   ```
   Reset Model space limits:
   Specify lower left corner or [ON/OFF] <0'-0",0'-0">:
   ⊞ ▾ LIMITS Specify upper right corner <1'-0",0'-9">: 60',40'
   Model   Layout1   Layout2   ✱                              1'-2", 0'-4 1
   ```

4. On your own, move the graphic cursor near the upper right corner inside the drawing area and note that the drawing area is unchanged. (The drawing limits command is used to set the drawing area, but the display will not be adjusted until a display related command is executed.)

5. In the *Menu Bar* area, select:

   [View] → [Zoom] → [All]

❖ The **Zoom All** command can be used to adjust the display so that all objects in the drawing are displayed to be as large as possible. If no objects are constructed, the **Drawing Limits** are used to adjust the current viewport.

6. Move the graphic cursor near the upper right corner inside the drawing area and note that the display area is updated.

GRID and *SNAP* Intervals Setup

1. In the *Menu Bar* area, select: **[Tools] → [Drafting Settings]**.

2. In the *Drafting Settings* dialog box, select the **SNAP and GRID** tab if it is not the page on top.

3. Change *Grid Spacing* to **6″** for both X and Y directions.

4. Also adjust the *Snap Spacing* to **6″** for both X and Y directions.

5. Pick **OK** to exit the *Drafting Settings* dialog box.

6. Move the cursor on top of the icons in the status toolbar and read the description of each icon. Note these icons act as toggle switches, which can be used to control the status of several commonly used *Display* and *Construction* options.

7. On your own, reset the option buttons so that *GRID DISPLAY, SNAP, ORTHO,* and *DYNAMIC INPUT* are switched *ON*.

Create Polylines

❖ In this tutorial, we will first create a 2D floor plan. The 2D floor plan will be converted into a 3D model with the **Thickness** command. In AutoCAD, a **polyline** is a connected sequence of line segments created as a single object. A polyline can contain straight line segments, arc segments, or a combination of the two.

1. Select the **Polyline** command icon in the *Draw* toolbar.

2. In the *command prompt area*, the message "*Specify start point:*" is displayed. Select a location that is near the coordinates (**25'-0"**, **10'-0"**) as the **starting point** of the *polyline*.

3. In the *command prompt area*, create a horizontal line by using the *relative rectangular coordinates entry method*, relative to the last point we specified. *Specify next point:* **@-11'6", 0 [ENTER]**.

4. In the *command prompt area*, create a vertical line by using the *relative rectangular coordinates entry method*, relative to the last point we specified. *Specify next point:* **@0, 25'6" [ENTER]**.

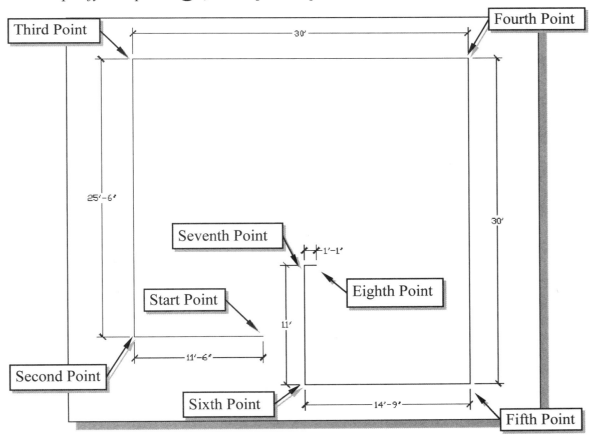

5. On your own, complete the polyline by specifying the rest of the points, *point four* through *point eight*.

6. Inside the *graphics window*, **right-click** and select **Enter** to end the Polyline command.

Create an Offset Polyline

- The **Offset** command creates a new object at a specified distance from an existing object or through a specified point.

1. Select the **Offset** command icon in the *Modify* toolbar. In the command prompt area, the message "*Specify offset distance or [Through]:*" is displayed.

Specify offset distance or [Through]]: **6″ [ENTER]**.

2. In the command prompt area, the message "*Select object to offset or <exit>:*" is displayed. Pick the polyline on the screen. (Note that all line segments of the polyline are automatically selected.)

3. AutoCAD next asks us to identify the direction of the offset. Pick a location that is **inside** the polyline.

4. Inside the graphics window, **right-click** and select **Enter** to end the Offset command.

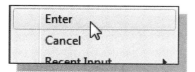

Create Interior Walls

1. In the *Menu Bar* area, choose **[Tools]** → **[Toolbars]** → **[AutoCAD]**

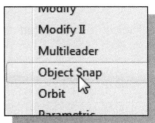

2. Select **Object Snap**, with the left-mouse-button, to display the *Object Snap* toolbar on the screen to assist the construction of the floor plan.

3. Select the **Polyline** command icon in the *Draw* toolbar. In the command prompt area, the message "*Specify start point or [Justification/ Scale/ Style]:*" is displayed.

4. In the *Object Snap* toolbar, pick **Snap to Midpoint**. In the command prompt area, the message "*_mid of*" is displayed. AutoCAD now expects us to select a geometric entity on the screen.

5. Select the vertical line on the left as shown.

6. At the *command prompt*, enter **@10′, 0 [ENTER]**.

7. On your own, define a vertical line at the location as shown in the figure.

8. Inside the graphics window, **right-click** and select **Enter** to end the Polyline command.

9. Select the **Offset** command icon in the *Modify* toolbar. In the command prompt area, the message *"Specify offset distance or [Through]:"* is displayed.

    Specify offset distance or [Through]]: 6" [**ENTER**].

10. In the command prompt area, the message *"Select object to offset or <exit>:"* is displayed. Pick the **polyline** we just created.

11. AutoCAD next asks us to identify the direction of the offset. Pick a location that is toward the *upper left* corner of the design.

12. Inside the graphics window, **right-click** to end the **Offset** command.

➢ In the *Status Bar* area, reset the option buttons and switch *OFF* all options.

- Next, we will create a 2'-8" doorway using the Snap From option.

13. Select the **Line** command icon in the *Draw* toolbar. In the command prompt area, the message "*_line Specify first point:*" is displayed.

❖ We will demonstrate the use of the Snap From option, which allows us to snap to any measurements of an existing location.

14. In the *Object Snap* toolbar, pick **Snap From**. In the command prompt area, the message "*_from Base point*" is displayed. AutoCAD now expects us to select a geometric entity on the screen.

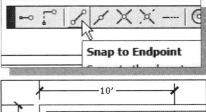

15. We will measure relative to the lower left corner of the interior wall. In the *Object Snap* toolbar, pick **Snap to Endpoint**.

16. In the command prompt area, the message "*_from Base point:_endp of*" is displayed. Pick **the lower right corner** as shown.

Lower-right corner

17. At the command prompt, enter **@0,1'-1"** [ENTER].

18. At the command prompt, enter **@-6", 0** [ENTER].

19. Inside the graphics window, right-click once and select **Enter** to end the Line command.

20. On your own, use the **Offset** command to create a parallel line that is **2'-8"** above the previous line.

Complete the Doorway Using the *Trim* Command

- The **Trim** command shortens an object so that it ends precisely at a selected boundary.

1. Select the **Trim** command icon in the *Modify* toolbar. In the command prompt area, the message "*Select boundary edges... Select objects:*" is displayed.

- First we will select the objects that define the boundary edges to which we want to trim the object.

2. Pick the **two horizontal lines** we just created as the *boundary edges*.

3. Inside the *graphics window*, **right-click** to proceed with the Trim command.

4. The message "*Select object to trim or shift-select object to extend or [Project/ Edge/ Undo]:*" is displayed in the command prompt area. Pick the vertical sections bound by the two selected horizontal lines.

5. Inside the graphics window, right-click to activate the option menu and select **Enter** with the left-mouse-button to end the Trim command.

- Using the Polyline and Line commands, create the additional walls and doorways as shown.

❖ Hints: Use the modify commands, such as **Trim/Extend** and **Erase** to assist the construction of the floor plan.

◆ Now is a good time to save the design. Select **[File]** → **[Save As]** in the pull-down menu and use *FloorPlan* as the *File name.*

User Coordinate System – It is an XY CRT, but an XYZ World

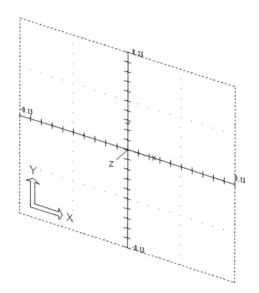

Design modeling software is becoming more powerful and user friendly, yet the system still does only what the user tells it to do. When using a geometric modeler, we therefore need to have a good understanding of what the inherent limitations are. We should also have a good understanding of what we want to do and what to expect, as the results are based on what is available.

In most 3D geometric modelers, 3D objects are located and defined in what is usually called **world space** or **global space**. Although a number of different coordinate systems can be used to create and manipulate objects in a 3D modeling system, the objects are typically defined and stored using the world space. The world space is usually a **3D Cartesian coordinate system** that the user cannot change or manipulate.

In most engineering designs, models can be very complex, and it would be tedious and confusing if only the world coordinate system were available. Practical 3D modeling systems allow the user to define **Local Coordinate Systems (LCS)** or **User Coordinate Systems (UCS)** relative to the world coordinate system. Once a local coordinate system is defined, we can then create geometry in terms of this more convenient system.

Although objects are created and stored in 3D space coordinates, most of the geometry entities can be referenced using 2D Cartesian coordinate systems. Typical input devices such as a mouse or digitizers are two-dimensional by nature; the movement of the input device is interpreted by the system in a planar sense. The same limitation is true of common output devices, such as CRT displays and plotters. The modeling software performs a series of three-dimensional to two-dimensional transformations to correctly project 3D objects onto a 2D picture plane.

The AutoCAD's **User Coordinate System (UCS)** is a special construction tool that enables the planar nature of the 2D input devices to be directly mapped into the 3D coordinate system. The **UCS** is a local coordinate system that can be aligned to the world coordinate system, an existing face of a part, or a predefined plane. By default, the UCS is aligned to the XY plane of the world coordinate system.

Think of the UCS as the surface on which we can sketch the 2D profiles of designs. It is similar to a piece of paper, a white board, or a chalkboard that can be attached to any planar surface. In the previous sections, we created the 2D design of a floor plan using the default settings where the UCS is aligned to the XY plane of the world coordinate system.

Viewing the 2D Design in 3D Space

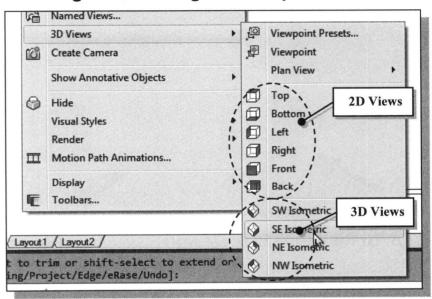

1. In the *Menu Bar* area, select:

   [View] →
   [3D Views] →
   [SE Isometric]

   - AutoCAD provides a set of pre-defined views, which contain most of the standard 2D and 3D views as shown in the figure.

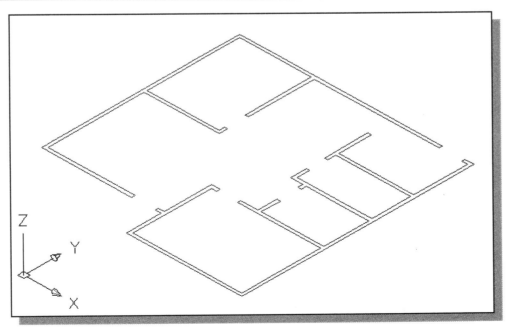

- The orientations of the preset 2D and 3D views are based on the world coordinate system as shown below. Note that the positive Y-axis direction is also identified as pointing toward **North** and the preset 3D views are oriented using the **North**, **East**, **South**, and **West** directions.

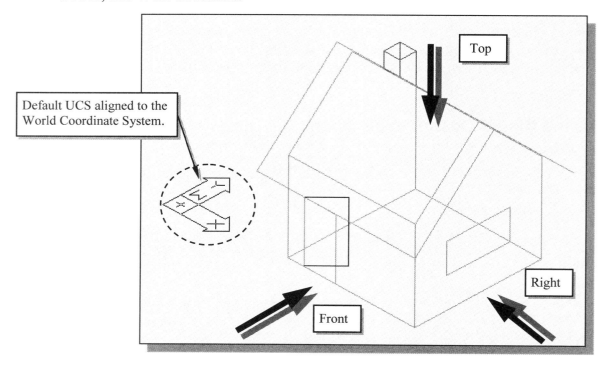

Default UCS aligned to the World Coordinate System.

Add the 3rd Dimension to the *Floor Plan* Design

❖ **AutoCAD® 2017** provides a flexible graphical user interface that allows users to select graphical entities **BEFORE** the command is selected (*Pre-selection*), or **AFTER** the command is selected (*Post-selection*). We can pre-select one or more objects by clicking on the objects at the command prompt (**Command:**). To deselect the selected items, press the **[Esc]** key twice.

1. Inside the graphics window, pre-select all objects by enclosing all objects inside a **selection window** as shown.

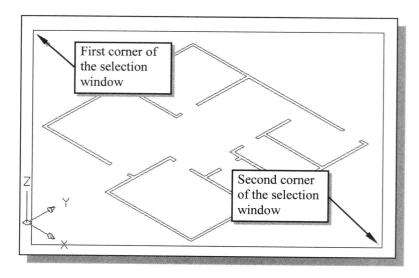

First corner of the selection window

Second corner of the selection window

2. Inside the graphics window, **right-click** once to bring up the option list and select **Properties** as shown.

3. In the *Properties* dialog box, properties of the highlighted entities are displayed. Notice the current *Thickness* is set to 0″.

4. **Left-click** the *Thickness* box and enter a new value **9′ [ENTER]** as the new thickness value.

5. Click on the [**X**] button to exit the *Properties* dialog box.

In AutoCAD, the *thickness* of an object determines the distance that the object is extruded above or below its current Z-elevation. Positive thickness will extrude the objects upward (positive Z), negative thickness extrudes downward (negative Z), and zero thickness means no extrusion. The Z direction is determined by the orientation of the UCS at the time the object was created.

Changing the *thickness* of objects will change the appearance of certain geometric objects, such as circles, lines, polylines, arcs, 2D solids, and points. Note that the *Thickness* property is not available on certain geometric objects, such as *Splines* and *Multilines*. We can set the *thickness* of an object with the ***Thickness*** variable. AutoCAD applies the extrusion uniformly to an object. A single object cannot have different thickness for its various points.

Changing the thickness of objects simulates a simple Z-extrusion of creating solid objects in AutoCAD. The main advantage of using the object thickness to create the Z-elevation instead of creating a true solid is that the operation is quick and easy. In AutoCAD, objects with thickness can be hidden, shaded, and rendered as if they are three-dimensional solids. Once an object's thickness is set, we can visualize the results in any view other than the plan view.

This method is also known as the **2½D solid modeling approach**. This modeling technique was first invented in the 1970s and was adopted by several of the first-generation solid-modeling packages. This approach requires no additional 3D construction tools and only minimum computing power is needed. Note that this modeling approach does not create true 3D solids and objects can only be extruded in one direction. This modeling approach is considered to be less flexible and its application is somewhat limited.

View the Design Using the Hide Option

- By default, AutoCAD produces a wireframe image of the constructed 2D/3D design on the screen. All geometric entities are present, including those that should be hidden by other objects. Several options are available in AutoCAD to create more realistic images of 3D designs. In this section, we will introduce the Hide option, which can be used to adjust the display of the design; the Hide option eliminates the hidden lines on the screen.

1. De-select any selected objects by hitting the [Esc] key once.

2. In the *pull-down menu*, click on the **View** option as shown.

3. Select the **[Visual Styles]** → **[Hidden]** option, the 3rd option in the list, as shown.

4. To redisplay the wireframe image, select the 1st option: **[2D WireFrame]**.

Add New Layers

1. In the *Menu Bar,* select **[Tools]** → **[Toolbars]** → **[AutoCAD]** → **[Layers]**.

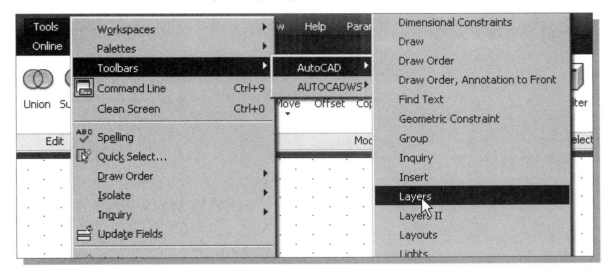

❖ The *Layer Properties Manager* dialog box appears. AutoCAD creates a default layer, *Layer 0*, which we cannot rename or delete. *Layer 0* has special properties used by the system.

2. Pick **Layers Properties Manager** in the *Layers* toolbar.

❖ In AutoCAD, we always construct entities on a layer. It may be the default layer or a layer that we create. Each layer has associated properties such as the visibility setting, color, linetype, lineweight, and plot style.

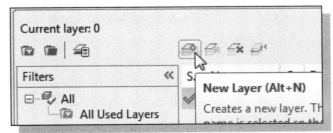

3. Click on the **New** button. Notice a layer is automatically added to the list of layers.

4. AutoCAD will assign a generic name to the new layer (*Layer1*). Enter **Walls** as the name of the new layer.

5. Pick the color swatch or the color name (**White**) of the *Walls* layer. The *Select Color* dialog box appears.

6. Select **Green** as the new layer color.

7. Click **OK** to accept the color setting.

8. On your own, create another layer (layer name: ***Roof***) and change the layer color to **Blue**.

9. Click on the **Set Current** button and make **Roof** the *Current Layer*. There can only be one *Current Layer*, and new entities are automatically placed on the layer that is set to be the *Current Layer*.

10. Click on the **Close** button to accept the settings.

Move Entities to a Different Layer

1. Inside the graphics window, pre-select all objects by enclosing all objects inside a **selection window**.

2. On the *Object Properties* toolbar, choose the ***Layer Control*** box with the left-mouse-button.

❖   Notice the layer name displayed in the *Layer Control* box is the selected object's assigned layer and layer properties.

3. In the *Layer Control* box, click on the ***Walls*** layer name. The selected objects are now moved to the *Walls* layer.

4. Press the [**Esc**] key to deselect the pre-selected objects.

5. On your own, confirm the ***Roof*** layer is set as the ***Current Layer***.

Reposition the UCS

*   AutoCAD's **User Coordinate System (UCS)** is a special construction tool that enables the planar nature of the 2D input devices to be directly mapped into the 3D coordinate system. The **UCS** is a local coordinate system that can be repositioned and/or reoriented to an existing face of a part or a predefined plane. By default, the UCS is aligned to the XY plane of the world coordinate system. Several options are available to reposition and reorient the UCS in 3D space.

1. In the *Menu Bar* area, select:

    [Tools] → [New UCS] → [Origin]

2. We will use the *Object Snap* and *Object Tracking* options to aid the repositioning of the UCS.

3. In the *Status Bar* area, reset the option buttons so that the *Dynamic Input, Polar Tracking, Object Snap, Object Snap Tracking* options are switched ***ON***.

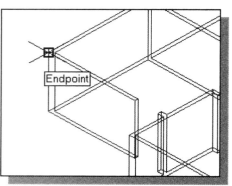

- We will reposition the UCS at the intersection of the left wall and the front wall; the intersection can be found by using the AutoCAD object tracking options.

4. Move the cursor on the top left corner of the external wall as shown; pause for a few seconds to activate the *OTRACK* option.

5. Move the cursor on the top front corner of the external wall as shown; pause for a few seconds to activate the *OTRACK* option.

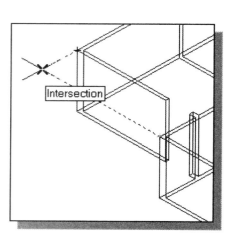

6. Left-click once when the cursor is aligned to the intersection of the left wall and the front wall as shown.

- The UCS is repositioned to the new location as shown. This location is the new origin for any geometric constructions.

Create the Roof

1. Select the **Rectangle** command icon in the *Draw* toolbar as shown.

2. In the command prompt area, the message "*Specify first corner point or [Chamfer/ Elevation/Fillet/ Thickness/Width]:*" is displayed. Move the cursor inside the graphics window and **right-click** to display the **option menu**.

*   The thickness of certain geometry entities can be set as they are being created.

3. In the *option menu*, select **Thickness** by clicking once with the left-mouse-button.

4. In the command prompt area, the message "*Specify thickness for rectangles <0'-0">:*" is displayed. Enter **10"** [ENTER].

5. At the command prompt, enter **-2',-2'** [ENTER].

6. In the command prompt area, the message "*Specify other corner point or [Dimensions]:*" is displayed. Enter **@34',34'** [ENTER].

*   Note that the coordinates entered are measured relative to the new UCS origin.

7. In the *View* pull-down menu, select *Visual Styles* then select:

[Hidden]

- The **Thickness** option extrudes the 2D design in the positive Z-direction relative to the current UCS, which is at the same Z-elevation of the plane of the 2D design. Note that the **Thickness** option only makes 2D objects look like 3D solids; only surfaces perpendicular to the plane of the 2D design are created. No top or bottom surfaces are created with the **Thickness** option.

8. Pick **Erase** in the *Modify* toolbar. (The icon is the first icon in the *Modify* toolbar.) The message "*Select objects*" is displayed in the command prompt area and AutoCAD awaits us to select the objects to erase.

9. Pick any edge of the **rectangle** we just created.

10. **Right-click** inside the graphics window to accept the selection.

11. Reset the display to the 2D wireframe image by using the *View* pull-down menu:

[Visual Styles] → [2D wireframe]

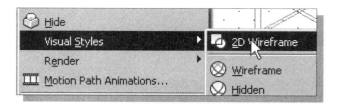

Rotating the UCS

- AutoCAD's **User Coordinate System (UCS)** can be repositioned and reoriented in 3D space. All of the UCS options are organized and can be found in the *Standard* toolbar.

  1. In the *Menu Bar* select **[Tools]** → **[Toolbars]** → **[AutoCAD]**.

  2. Select **UCS**, with the left-mouse-button, to display the *UCS* toolbar on the screen to assist the construction of the *Roof*.

  3. Select the **X Axis Rotate** option in the *UCS* toolbar as shown.

  4. In the command prompt area, the message "*Specify rotation angle about X axis<90>:*" is displayed. Enter **90** [**ENTER**].

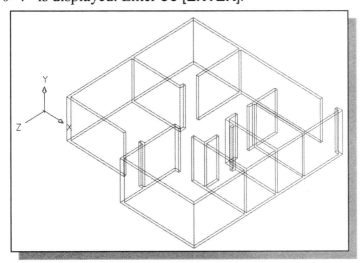

- The UCS rotation is done using the standard engineering convention, where positive values are treated as rotating counterclockwise. Also note that the *SNAP*, *GRID*, and *ORTHO* options all rotate in line with the UCS.

Sketching on the Rotated UCS

1. Select the **Rectangle** command icon in the *Draw* toolbar as shown.

2. Move the cursor inside the graphics window and right-click to display the option menu.

3. In the *option menu*, select **Thickness** by clicking once with the left-mouse-button.

4. In the *command prompt* area, the message *"Specify thickness for rectangles <0'-10">:"* is displayed. Enter **-34'** [**ENTER**].

5. At the *command prompt*, enter **-2',0',2'** [**ENTER**] as the first corner of the rectangle. (Note the z-coordinate input.)

6. In the *command prompt* area, the message *"Specify other corner point or [Dimensions]:"* is displayed. Enter **@36',10"** [**ENTER**].

* The negative thickness extrudes the rectangle in the negative Z-direction of the current UCS.

View the Design Using the Hidden Option

- Several options are available in AutoCAD to create more realistic images of 3D designs. The **Visual Styles - Hidden** option can also be used to eliminate the hidden lines on the screen. The **Visual Styles - Hidden** option performs a more complicated calculation of the display and usually produces a better image than the **Hide** option.

1. In the *View* toolbar panel, select:

   [Visual Styles] →
   [Hidden]

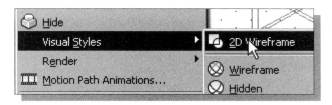

2. To display the 2D wireframe image, select:

   [Visual Styles] →
   [2D Wireframe]

Review Questions:

1. What is the difference between *WCS* and *UCS*?

2. List and describe two available options to manipulate the UCS.

3. Describe some of the advantages of using the AutoCAD **Thickness** option over creating 2D or 3D models.

4. In the tutorial, which commands were used to eliminate the hidden lines on the screen?

5. What is the difference between a Polyline and a Line?

6. Identify the following commands:

(a)

(b)

(c)

(d)

Exercises:

1.   Dimensions are in inches. Thickness: Base 0.25

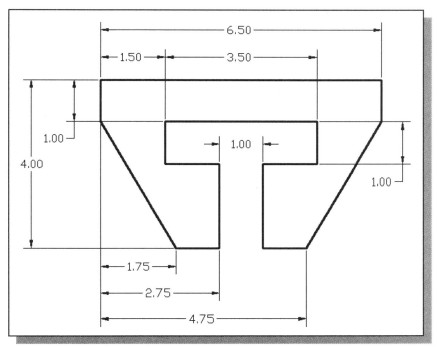

2.   Wall thickness: 5 inches; height: 10 feet

3.   Dimensions are in inches. Thickness: 0.25

4.   Dimensions are in inches. Thickness: 0.25

Chapter 3
3D Wireframe Modeling

Learning Objectives

- ◆ **Use the Setup Wizard**
- ◆ **Create Wireframe Models**
- ◆ **Apply the Box Method in Creating Models**
- ◆ **Construct with the Copy Command**
- ◆ **Understand the Available 3D Coordinates Input Options**
- ◆ **Use the View Toolbar**
- ◆ **Set up and Use the TRIM options**

Introduction

The first true 3D computer model created on CAD systems in the late 1970s was the 3D wireframe model. Computer generated 3D wireframe models contain information about the locations of all the corners and edges in space coordinates. The 3D wireframe models can be viewed from any direction as needed and are in general reasonably good representations of 3D design. But because surface definition is not part of a wireframe model, all wireframe images have the inherent problem of ambiguity. For example, in the figure displayed below, which corner is in front, corner A or corner B? The ambiguity problem becomes much more serious with complex designs that have many edges and corners.

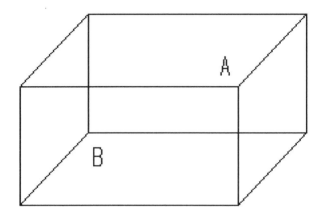

Wireframe Ambiguity: Which corner is in front, A or B?

The main advantage of using a 3D wireframe modeler to create 3D models is its simplicity. The computer hardware requirements for wireframe modelers are typically much lower than the requirements for surface and solid modelers. A 3D wireframe model, also known as a stick-figure model or a skeleton model, contains only information about the locations of all the corners and edges of the design in space coordinates. You should also realize that, in some cases, it could be quite difficult to locate some of the corner locations while creating a 3D wireframe model. Note that 3D wireframe modelers are usually used in conjunction with surfacing modelers, which we will discuss in the later chapters of this text, to eliminate the problem of ambiguity.

With most CAD systems, creating 3D wireframe models usually starts with constructing 2D entities in 3D space. Two of the most commonly used methods for creating 3D wireframe models are the **Box method** and the **2D Extrusion method**. As the name implies, the *Box method* involves the creation of a 3D box with the edges constructed from the overall height, width and depth dimensions of the design. The 3D wireframe model is typically completed by locating and connecting corners within the box.

The *2D Extrusion method* involves making copies of 2D geometries in specific directions. This method is similar to the 2½D extrusion approach illustrated in the previous chapter (Chapter 2) with several differences. First of all, we do not really extrude the wireframe entities; instead we simply make copies of wireframe entities in the desired directions. Secondly, constructed wireframe entities have true 3D space coordinates, while the *thickness* approach creates entities with no true 3D coordinates. Finally, no surfaces are created in the 3D wireframe models.

In this chapter, we will illustrate the general procedure to construct a 3D wireframe model using both the box method and the 2D extrusion method. To illustrate the AutoCAD 3D construction environment, we will create the wireframe model using only the default UCS system, which is aligned to the world coordinate system. Repositioning and/or reorienting the User Coordinate System can be useful in creating 3D models. However, it is also feasible to create 3D models referencing only a single coordinate system. One important note about creating wireframe models is that the construction techniques mostly concentrate on locating the space coordinates of the individual corners of the design. The ability to visualize designs in the form of 3D wireframe models is extremely helpful to designers and CAD operators. It is hoped that the experience of thinking and working on 3D wireframe models, as outlined in this chapter, will enhance one's 3D visualization ability.

The *Locator* Design

Starting Up AutoCAD 2017

1. Start **AutoCAD 2017** by selecting the *Autodesk* folder in the **Start** menu as shown. Once the program is loaded into the memory, click **Start Drawing** to start a new drawing.

Activate the Startup Option

❖ In **AutoCAD 2017**, we can use the *Startup* dialog box to establish different types of drawing settings. The *Startup* dialog box can be activated through the use of the **STARTUP** system variable.

The STARTUP system variable can be set to 0, 1, 2 or 3:
*   1: displays the ***Create New Drawing*** dialog box.
*   0: displays the ***Select Template*** dialog box (default).
*   2: Displays the ***Start Tab*** with options; a custom dialog box can be used.
*   3: Displays the ***Start Tab*** with the ribbon pre-loaded (default).

1. In the *command prompt area*, enter the system variable name:

    STARTUP [ENTER]

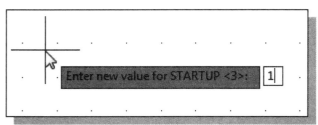

2. Enter **1** as the new value for the **STARTUP** system variable.

3. To show the effect of the *Startup* option, **exit** AutoCAD by clicking on the **Close** icon as shown.

4. Restart AutoCAD by selecting the **AutoCAD 2017** option through the *Start* menu.

5. The *Startup* dialog box appears on the screen with different options to assist the creation of drawings. Move the cursor on top of the four icons and notice the four options available:
   (1) **Open a Drawing**
   (2) **Start from Scratch**
   (3) **Use a Template** and
   (4) **Use a Setup Wizard**.

6. In the *Startup* dialog box, select the **Start from Scratch** option as shown in the figure.

7. Choose **Imperial** to use the *Standard English* units setting.

8. Click **OK** to accept the setting.

Create the Rectangular Base of the Design

➢ We will first construct the wireframe geometry defining the rectangular base of the design.

    1. In the *Status Bar* area, reset the options and turn ***ON*** the *Grid Display, Polar Tracking, Object Snap, Object Snap Tracking, Dynamic Input* and *Lineweight* options.

    2. Select the **Rectangle** icon in the *Draw* toolbar.

    3. Place the first corner-point of the rectangle at the origin of the world coordinate system.
Command: _line Specify first point:
0,0 [ENTER].
       (Type **0,0** and press the [**ENTER**] key once.)

    4. We will create a 4.5″ × 3.0″ rectangle by entering the absolute coordinates of the second corner.
Specify other corner point or [Dimension]: **4.5,3 [ENTER]**.

• The Rectangle command creates rectangles as *polyline* features, which means the four segments of a rectangle are created as a single object. In AutoCAD, rectangles are wireframe entities.

5. In the *Menu Bar*, select:
    [View] → [3D Views] → [SE Isometric]

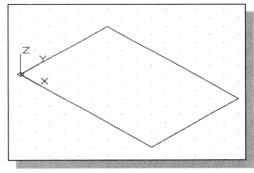

• Notice the orientation of the sketched 2D rectangle in relation to the displayed AutoCAD user coordinate system. By default, the 2D sketch-plane is aligned to the XY plane of the world coordinate system.

Create a 3D Box

• We will create a 3D box to define the 3D boundary of the design. We will do so by placing a copy of the base rectangle at the corresponding height elevation of the design. The dimensions of the 3D box are therefore based on the height, width and depth dimensions of the design.

1. Click on the **Copy Object** icon in the *Modify* toolbar.

2. In the command prompt area, the message "*Select objects:*" is displayed. Pick any edge of the sketched rectangle.

3. Inside the graphics window, right-click once to accept the selection.

4. In the command prompt area, the message "*Specify base point or displacement, or [Multiple]:*" is displayed. Pick any **corner** of the sketched **rectangle** as a base point to create the copy.

5. In the command prompt area, the message "*Specify second point of displacement or <use first point as displacement>:*" is displayed.
    Enter **@0,0,2.5 [ENTER]**.
    (The three values are the X, Y and Z coordinates of the new location.)

6. Select the **[Zoom Extents]** option in the *View* pull-down menu to view the constructed geometry.

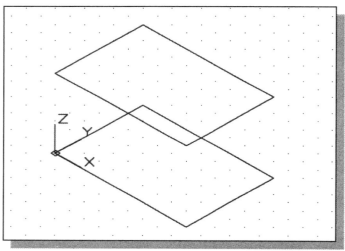

❖ The two rectangles represent the top and bottom of a 3D box defining the 3D boundary of the design. Note that the construction of the second rectangle was independent of the UCS, *User Coordinate System*; the UCS is still aligned to the *world coordinate system.*

7. Select the **Line** icon in the *Draw* toolbar.

8. In the command prompt area, the message "*_line Specify first point:*" is displayed.
    Command: _line Specify first point:
    0,0 [ENTER]

9. In the command prompt area, the message "*Specify next point or [Undo]:*" is displayed.
    Command: _line Specify first point: **0,0,2.5 [ENTER]**.

❖ Notice the Line command correctly identified the entered 3D coordinates of the second point. The default Z-coordinate, which is set by the AutoCAD UCS, is applied automatically whenever the Z-coordinates are omitted.

10. Inside the graphics window, right-click to activate the option menu and select **Enter** with the left-mouse-button to end the Line command.

11. Inside the graphics window, **right-click** to bring up the pop-up option menu.

12. Pick **Repeat Line** with the left-mouse-button in the pop-up menu to repeat the last command.

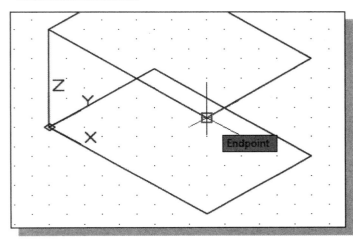

13. Move the cursor on top of the top front corner as shown. Note that AutoCAD's *Object Snap* and *Object Snap Tracking* features identify geometric features, such as endpoints, automatically.

14. Left-click once to select the endpoint as shown in the above figure.

15. Create a line connecting to the endpoint directly below the previously selected point.

16. On your own, complete the 3D box by creating the two lines connecting the back corners of the 3D box as shown.

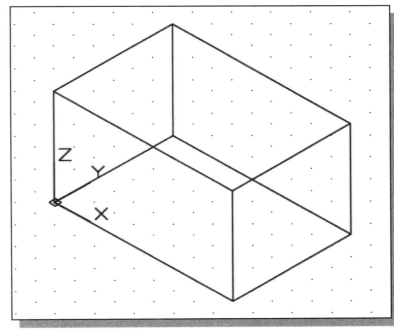

Object Snap Toolbar

1. In the *Menu Bar* select **[Tools]** → **[Toolbars]** → **[AutoCAD]**.

❖ AutoCAD provides many toolbars for access to frequently used commands, settings, and modes. The *Standard*, *Object Properties*, *Draw*, and *Modify* toolbars are displayed by default. The *check marks* in the list identify the toolbars that are currently displayed on the screen.

2. Select **Object Snap**, with the left-mouse-button, to display the *Object Snap* toolbar on the screen to assist the construction of the design.

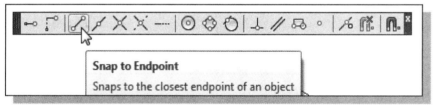

❖ *Object Snap* is an extremely powerful construction tool available on most CAD systems. During an entity's creation operations, we can snap the cursor to points on objects such as endpoints, midpoints, centers, and intersections. For example, we can turn on *Object Snap* and quickly draw a line to the center of a circle, the midpoint of a line segment, or the intersection of two lines.

Use the Snap Options to Locate the Top Corners

❖ We will use the *Object Snap* options to identify the locations of the top corners of the model.

1. Select the **Line** icon in the *Draw* toolbar.

2. In the command prompt area, the message "*_line Specify first point:*" is displayed. Select **Snap From** in the *Object Snap* toolbar.

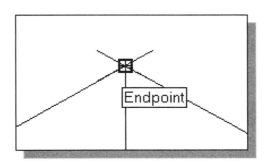

3. Select the **top back corner** as the reference point as shown.

4. In the command prompt area, the message "*_line Specify first point: from Base point:<Offset>:*" is displayed.

   Command: **@0.75,0,0 [ENTER]**.

❖ By using the relative coordinate input method, we can locate the position of any point in 3D space. Note that the entered coordinates are measured relative to the current UCS.

5. In the command prompt area, the message "*Specify next point or [Undo]:*" is displayed.
   Command: Specify next point or [Undo]: **@0,-2,0 [ENTER]**.

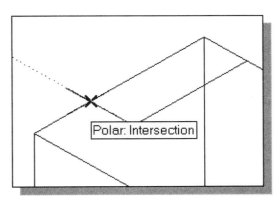

6. Move the cursor toward the left to create a perpendicular line. Select a location that is on the back line as shown; notice the displayed *Object Snap/Tracking* tips: Polar: Intersection.

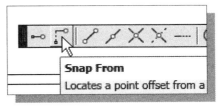

7. In the command prompt area, the message "*Specify next point or [Undo]:*" is displayed. Select **Snap From** in the *Object Snap* toolbar.

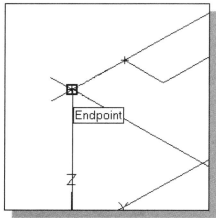

8. Select the **top front corner** as the reference point as shown.

9. In the command prompt area, the message "*Specify next point or [Close/Undo]:_from Base point <Offset>:*" is displayed.

    Command: **@0,0,-1 [ENTER]**.

10. In the command prompt area, the message "*Specify next point or [Undo]:*" is displayed.
    Command: **@0.75,0,0 [ENTER]**.

11. Move the cursor to the top corner as shown in the figure.

❖ Using the *Object Snap* options and the *relative coordinate input method* allow us to quickly locate points in 3D space.

12. Inside the graphics window, right-click to activate the option menu and select **Enter** with the left-mouse-button to end the Line command.

Use the *Copy* Option to Create Additional Edges

❖ The Copy option can also be used to create additional edges of the wireframe model.

1. Click on the **Copy Object** icon in the *Modify* toolbar.

2. In the command prompt area, the message "*Select objects:*" is displayed. Pick **any edge** of the bottom rectangle.

3. Inside the graphics window, **right-click** once to accept the selection.

4. In the *command prompt area*, the message "*Specify base point or displacement, or [Multiple]:*" is displayed. Pick **any corner** of the base rectangle to be used as a base point to create the copy.

5. In the *command prompt area*, the message "*Specify second point of displacement or <use first point as displacement>:*" is displayed.
    Enter **@0,0,0.75 [ENTER]**.

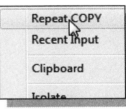

6. Inside the graphics window, right-click to bring up the pop-up option menu.

7. Pick **Repeat Copy Object** with the left-mouse-button in the pop-up menu to repeat the last command.

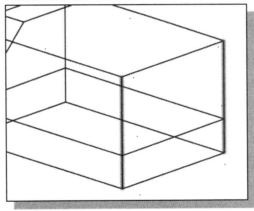

8. Pick the two **vertical lines** on the right side of the 3D box as shown.

9. Inside the graphics window, **right-click** once to accept the selection.

10. In the command prompt area, the message "*Specify base point or displacement, or [Multiple]:*" is displayed. Pick the **top back corner** of the wireframe as a base point to create the copy.

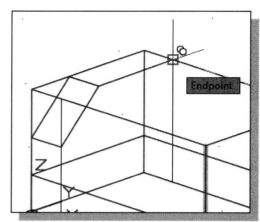

❖ The copy option is an effective way to create additional edges of wireframe models, especially when multiple objects are involved. With wireframe models, the emphasis is placed on the corners and edges of the model.

11. In the command prompt area, the message "*Specify second point of displacement or <use first point as displacement>:*" is displayed. Pick the **top back corner** of the wireframe model as shown.

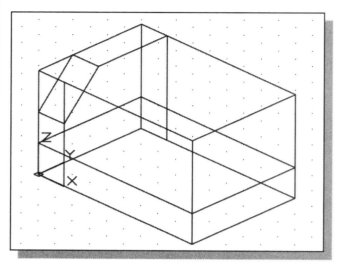

Use the Trim Command

❖ The Trim command can be used to shorten objects so that they end precisely at selected boundaries.

1. Select the **Trim** command icon in the *Modify* toolbar. In the command prompt area, the message "*Select boundary edges... Select objects:*" is displayed.

❖ First we will select the objects that define the boundary edges to which we want to trim the object.

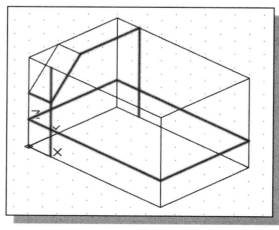

2. Pick the highlighted edges as shown in the figure; these edges are the *boundary edges*.

3. Inside the graphics window, **right-click** once to accept the selection of boundary edges and proceeds with the Trim command.

4. Inside the graphics area, right-click once to bring up the option menu and select **Project** as shown.

5. Inside the graphics area, right-click once to bring up the option menu and select **View** to allow trimming option based on the displayed view.

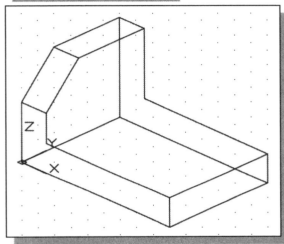

6. The message "*Select object to trim or shift-select object to extend or [Project/Edge/Undo]:*" is displayed in the command prompt area. Pick the portions of the entities to be trimmed so that the model appears as shown.

❖ Note that in AutoCAD 2017, the default AutoCAD trim projection setting is set to **UCS**, which allows us to trim objects that are perpendicular to the **UCS plane**.

7. Inside the graphics window, right-click to bring up the option menu and select **Enter** to end the Trim command.

8. On your own, use the **Line** command to complete the inside corner of the wireframe model as shown.

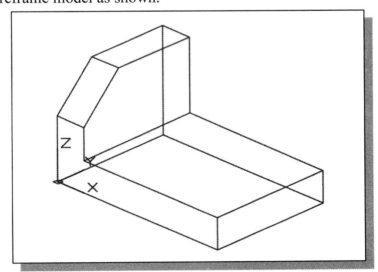

Use the View Toolbar

1. In the *Menu Bar* select **[Tools]** → **[Toolbars]** → **[AutoCAD]**.

2. Select **View**, with the left-mouse-button, to display the *View* toolbar on the screen.

➢ The *View* toolbar contains two sections of icons that allow us to quickly switch to standard 2D and 3D views.

Dynamic Rotation – Free Orbit

1. Select **Free Orbit** in the *View* pull-down menu:

    [Orbit] → **[Free Orbit]**

❖ The Free Orbit view displays an ***arcball***, which enables us to manipulate the view of 3D objects by clicking and dragging with the left-mouse-button.

2. Inside the *arcball*, press down the left-mouse-button and drag it up and down to rotate about the screen X-axis. Dragging the mouse left and right will rotate about the screen Y-axis.

3. Move the cursor to different locations on the screen, outside the *arcball* or on one of the four small circles, and experiment with the real-time dynamic rotation feature of the **Free Orbit** command.

Use the *Offset* Command to Create Parallel Edges

❖ The AutoCAD **Offset** option can also be used to create edges that are at specific distances to existing 3D wireframe edges. Prior to creating the parallel edges, we will first convert one of the polylines to individual line segments.

1. Pick the top right edge of the wireframe model.

• **AutoCAD 2017** provides a flexible graphical user interface that allows users to select graphical entities BEFORE the command is selected (*Pre-selection*), or AFTER the command is selected (*Post-selection*). The polyline we have pre-selected consists of three line-segments.

2. Select the **Explode** command in the *Modify* pull-down menu as shown.

3. Pick **Offset** in the *Modify* toolbar as shown.

4. In the command prompt area, the message "*Specify offset distance or [Through] <Through>:*" is displayed. Enter **0.5 [ENTER]**.

5. Select the front line segment of the polyline we just exploded.

6. In the command prompt area, the message "*Specify point on side to offset:*" is displayed. Pick a location that is above the line to create the first parallel line.

7. Select the back line segment of the polyline we exploded and create another parallel line as shown.

8. On your own, repeat the above steps and create another parallel line (distance: **1.5**) as shown.

- In creating parallel edges, the **Offset** command can be viewed as an alternative to the **Copy** command. In 3D wireframe modeling, the focus is on identifying the edges and corners of the model. Most of the 2D construction tools are also applicable in a 3D environment.

9. Select the **Trim** command icon in the *Modify* toolbar.

10. In the command prompt area, the message "*Select boundary edges... Select objects:*" is displayed. Pick the highlighted edges as shown in the figure; these edges are the *boundary edges*.

11. Inside the graphics window, right-click to accept the selection of boundary edges and proceeds with the **Trim** command.

12. On your own, trim the line segments so that the wireframe model appears as shown.

Create a Circle above the UCS Sketch Plane

1. Select the **Circle** command icon in the *Draw* toolbar.

   • By default, the XY plane of the UCS defines the sketching plane for constructing 2D geometric entities.

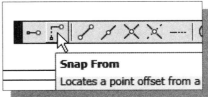

2. In the command prompt area, the message "*_circle Specify center point for circle or[3P/2P/Ttr (tan tan radius)]:*" is displayed. Select **Snap From** in the *Object Snap* toolbar.

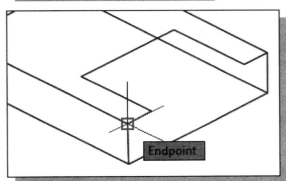

3. Select the **top right corner** as the reference point as shown.

4. In the command prompt area, the message "*Specify next point or [Close/Undo]:_from Base point <Offset>:*" is displayed.

   Command: **@-2.67,1.5 [ENTER]**.

5. In the command prompt area, the message "*Specify radius of circle or [Diameter]:*" is displayed.

   Command: **0.375 [ENTER]**.

   • The circle is created above the sketching plane with the **Snap From** option.

Complete the Wireframe Model

1. Click on the **Copy Object** icon in the *Modify* toolbar.

2. In the command prompt area, the message "*Select objects:*" is displayed. Pick the edges and the circle as shown in the figure.

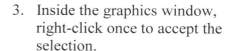

3. Inside the graphics window, right-click once to accept the selection.

4. In the command prompt area, the message "*Specify base point or displacement, or [Multiple]:*" is displayed. Pick the front right corner as shown.

5. In the command prompt area, the message "*Specify second point of displacement or <use first point as displacement>:*" is displayed. Pick the bottom-right corner as shown.

6. Select the **Line** icon in the *Draw* toolbar.

7. On your own, create the lines connecting the corners of the created edges as shown in the figure below.

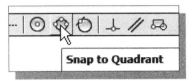

8. Use the **Snap to Quadrant** option to create edges in between the two circles.

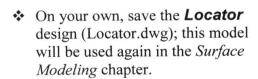

9. Select the **Trim** command icon in the *Modify* toolbar.

10. On your own, trim the center portion of the bottom right edge and complete the wireframe model as shown.

❖ On your own, save the **Locator** design (Locator.dwg); this model will be used again in the *Surface Modeling* chapter.

Review Questions:

1. Describe some of the control options available with the **Free Orbit** command.

2. List and describe two different methods to create 3D edges from existing 3D edges in **AutoCAD® 2017**.

3. How many of the UCS options were used to create the 3D model in this chapter and how many were used to create the model in the previous chapter?

4. When and why would you use the **Trim-Project-View** option?

5. Identify the following commands:

(a)

(b)

(c)

(d)

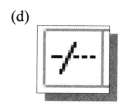

Exercises: All dimensions are in inches.

1. Thickness: Base **0.25** inches. Boss height **0.125** inches.
    The two diameter 1.00 holes are through holes.

2.

3.

4.

5.

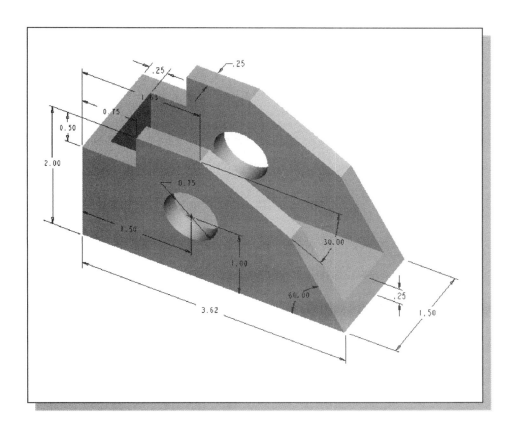

Notes:

Chapter 4
UCS, Viewports and Wireframe Modeling

Learning Objectives

♦ **Understand the Use of UCS on More Complex Designs**

♦ **Display and Orient 3D Views**

♦ **Apply and Expand the Basic Wireframe Construction Techniques**

♦ **Use Additional Tools to Assist the Creation of 3D Wireframe Models**

♦ **Use the Named Views Option**

Introduction

In the previous chapter, we examined some of the basic techniques to create 3D wireframe models. Again, a wireframe model is a skeletal description of a 3D object. There are no surfaces in a wireframe model; it consists only of points, lines, and curves that describe the edges of the object.

In this chapter, we will further discuss the techniques and wireframe modeling tools available in AutoCAD. Instead of creating the corners and edges of wireframe models by entering the precise 3D coordinates, the use of construction lines and referencing techniques are illustrated. The construction of edges in 3D space can be simplified by using the *AutoCAD* User Coordinate System. We will also use the multiple viewports option, which is available in most CAD systems, to aid the construction of 3D wireframe models.

It is important to point out that most of the construction tools used in creating 2D designs, such as *Object Snap* and *Polar Tracking*, as well as the Copy, Mirror, and Array commands, are also applicable to the constructions of 3D wireframe models.

The *V-Block* Design

Starting Up AutoCAD 2017

1. Select the **AutoCAD 2017** option on the *Program* menu or select the **AutoCAD 2017** icon on the *Desktop*.

2. In the *Startup* window, select **Start from Scratch**.

3. In the *Default Settings* section, pick **Imperial (feet and inches)** as the drawing units.

   4. Pick **OK** in the *Startup* dialog box to accept the selected settings.

3D Modeling Workspace

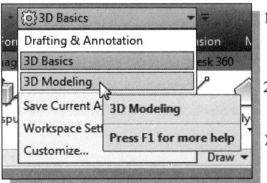

1. Click on the workspaces list in the *Quick Access* toolbar and choose to use the **3D Modeling** workspace as shown.

2. On your own, close any of the displayed palettes and switch on the **Menu Bar**.

➢ Notice the different 3D modeling toolbars available in the *Ribbon* toolbar area as shown.

Layers Setup

1. In the *Menu Bar,* select **[Tools]** → **[Toolbars]** → **[AutoCAD]** → **[Layers]**.

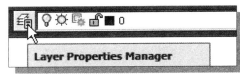

2. Click **Layer Properties Manager** in the *Layers* toolbar.

❖ In AutoCAD, we always construct entities on a layer. It may be the default layer or a layer that we create. Each layer has associated properties such as the visibility setting, color, linetype, lineweight, and plot style.

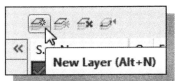

3. Click on the **New Layer** button. Notice a layer is automatically added to the list of layers.

4. Create **two new layers** with the following settings:

Layer	Color	Linetype	Lineweight
Construction	Grey	Continuous	Default
Object	Cyan	Continuous	0.30mm

5. Highlight the layer *Construction* in the list of layers.

6. Click on the **Current** icon to set layer *Construction* as the *Current Layer.*

7. Click on the **Close** button to accept the settings and exit the *Layer Properties Manager* dialog box.

8. In the *Status Bar* area, turn *ON* the *Grid Display, Polar Tracking, Object Snap, Object Snap Tracking, Dynamic Input* and *Lineweight* options.

Create the Rectangular Base of the Design

➤ We will first use construction geometry to define the outer edges of the design.

1. In the *Layer Control* box, confirm that layer *Construction* is set as the *Current Layer*.

2. Select the **Rectangle** icon in the *Draw* toolbar. In the command prompt area, the message "*Specify first corner point or [Chamfer/Elevation/Fillet/ Thickness/ Width]:*" is displayed.

3. Place the first corner point of the rectangle near the lower left corner of the screen. Do not be overly concerned about the actual coordinates of the location; the drawing space is as big as you can imagine.

4. We will create a 3″ × 2″ rectangle by entering the coordinates of the second corner using the relative coordinates input method.
   Specify other corner point or [Dimension]: **@3,2 [ENTER]**.

5. In the *View* panel, select:

   [Unsaved View] → [SE Isometric]

- Notice the orientation of the sketched 2D rectangle in relation to the displayed AutoCAD user coordinate system. By default, the 2D sketch-plane is aligned to the XY plane of the world coordinate system.

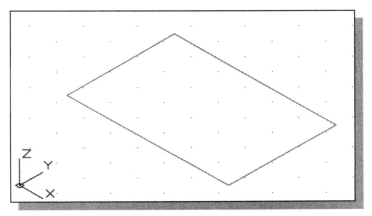

Create a Wireframe Box

- Next, we will use the Copy command to define the 3D boundary of the design.

1. Click on the **Copy Object** icon in the *Modify* toolbar.

2. In the command prompt area, the message *"Select objects:"* is displayed. Pick any edge of the sketched rectangle.

3. Inside the graphics window, right-click once to accept the selection.

4. In the command prompt area, the message *"Specify base point or displacement, or [Multiple]:"* is displayed. Pick any corner of the sketched rectangle as a base point to create the copy.

5. In the command prompt area, the message *"Specify second point of displacement or <use first point as displacement>:"* is displayed.
   Enter **@0,0,2.25 [ENTER]**.

➢ Note that the three values represent the distance measured in the X, Y and Z directions relative to the current UCS.

6. Use the **Zoom All** command, in the *View Display* toolbar, to adjust the display.

7. On your own, use the **Line** command to create the four lines connecting the four-corners of the two rectangles as shown.

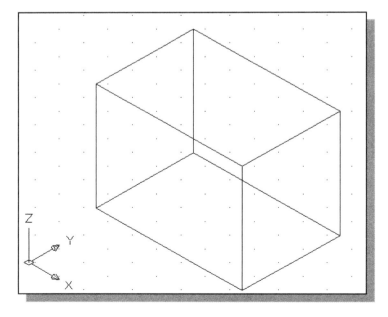

Using the View and UCS Toolbars

1. In the *Menu Bar,* select **[Tools]** → **[Toolbars]** → **[AutoCAD]**.

2. Select **View**, with the left-mouse-button, to display the *View* toolbar on the screen.

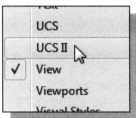

3. Move the cursor to the *Standard* toolbar area and **right-click** on any icon of the *Standard* toolbar to display a list of toolbar menu groups.

4. Select **UCS II**, with the left-mouse-button, to display the *UCSII* toolbar on the screen.

➢ The options available in *UCS II* toolbar allow us to quickly align the UCS to the preset standard 2D views.

5. Note that the current *UCS* is aligned to the *World Coordinate System.* Select **Front** in the *UCS II* toolbar as shown.

➢ Note that the UCS has been adjusted and it is now aligned parallel to the front view of the wireframe box as shown in the figure.

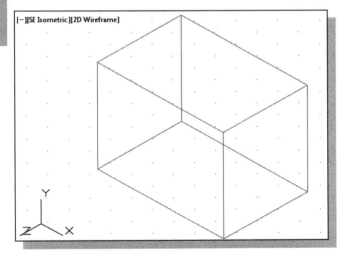

Create Construction Lines in the Front View

1. Select the **Line** command icon in the *Draw* toolbar. In the command prompt area, the message "*_line Specify first point:*" is displayed.

2. Inside the graphics window, hold down the **[SHIFT]** key and **right-click** once to bring up the *Object Snap* shortcut menu.

3. Select the **From** option in the pop-up window.

4. Pick the lower right corner of the bottom horizontal line in the front view as the base point.

5. In the command prompt area, the message "*Specify next point or [Undo]:*" is displayed. Enter **@0,0.75 [ENTER]**.

6. We will set up the *Polar Tracking* option to assist the creation of the next corner. **Right-click** once on the *POLAR* Tracking option located at the bottom of the graphics window.

7. In the option menu, select **Settings** by clicking once with the left-mouse-button.

8. In the *Drafting Settings* dialog box, set the *Polar Increment Angle* setting to **30** degrees.

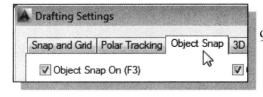

9. Click on the **Object Snap** tab to switch to the *Object Snap* option settings.

10. Confirm that the *Intersection* and *Extension* options are switched *ON* as shown.

11. Click on the **OK** button to accept the settings.

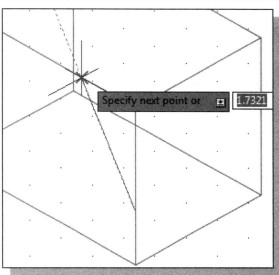

12. In the command prompt area, the message "*Specify next point or [Undo]:*" is displayed. Using the *Polar Tracking* option (30 degrees increment), create a line as shown in the figure.

13. Move the cursor near the left vertical edge of the front view and create the second line perpendicular to the last line we created.

14. Inside the graphics window, **right-click** to activate the option menu and select **Enter** with the left-mouse-button to end the Line command.

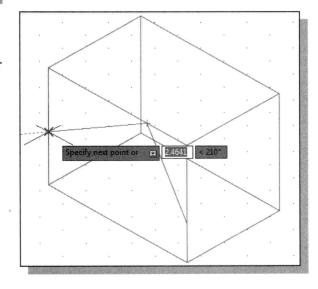

Copy Objects in the Negative Z Direction

1. Click on the **Copy Object** icon in the *Modify* toolbar.

2. In the command prompt area, the message "*Select objects:*" is displayed. Pick the two edges we just created.

3. Inside the graphics window, right-mouse-click once to accept the selection.

4. In the command prompt area, the message "*Specify base point or displacement, or [Multiple]:*" is displayed. Pick any **corner** of the wireframe model to use as a base point to create the copy.

5. In the command prompt area, the message "*Specify second point of displacement or <use first point as displacement>:*" is displayed.

    Enter **@0,0,-2.0 [ENTER]**.

➢ Note that the negative value represents the distance measured in the negative Z direction relative to the current UCS.

6. On your own, create three lines to connect the corners of the two sets of lines we just created, as shown below.

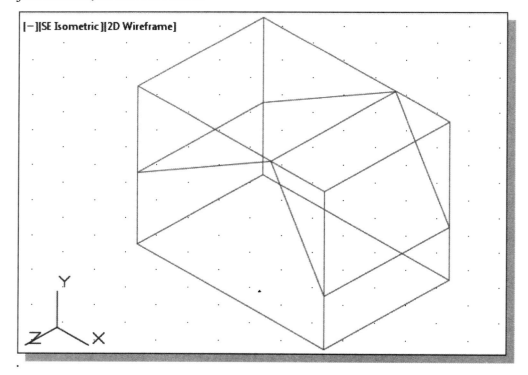

Create an Inclined Line at the Base of the Model

1. Select **Top** in the *UCS II* toolbar as shown.

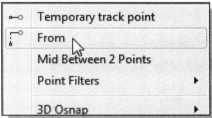

2. Select the **Line** command icon in the *Draw* toolbar. In the command prompt area, the message "*_line Specify first point:*" is displayed.

3. Inside the graphics window, hold down the [**SHIFT**] key and **right-click** once to bring up the *Object Snap* shortcut menu.

4. Select the **From** option in the pop-up window.

5. Pick the lower right corner of the bottom horizontal line as the base point as shown in the figure.

6. We will place the first point above the selected corner. Enter **@0,0.75 [ENTER]**.

7. In the command prompt area, the message "*Specify next point or [Undo]:*" is displayed. Using the *Polar Tracking* option (30 degrees increment), create a line as shown in the figure.

8. Inside the *graphics window*, **right-click** to activate the option menu and select **Enter** with the left-mouse-button to end the Line command.

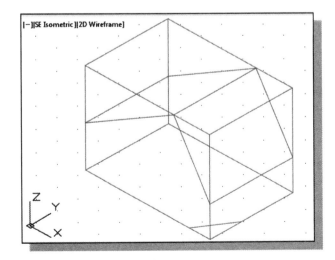

➢ On your own, use the **Copy** and **Line** commands to create additional edges so that the wireframe model appears as shown below.

Create Object Lines

1. On the *Object Properties* toolbar, choose the **Layer Control** box with the left-mouse-button.

2. Move the cursor over the name of layer **Object**; the tool tip "*Object*" appears.

3. **Left-click once** on the layer name and now layer *Object* is set as the *Current Layer*.

4. Select the **Line** command icon in the *Draw* toolbar. In the command prompt area, the message "*_line Specify first point:*" is displayed.

5. Pick the lower left corner of the bottom of the wireframe model as the starting point and create the four line segments as shown.

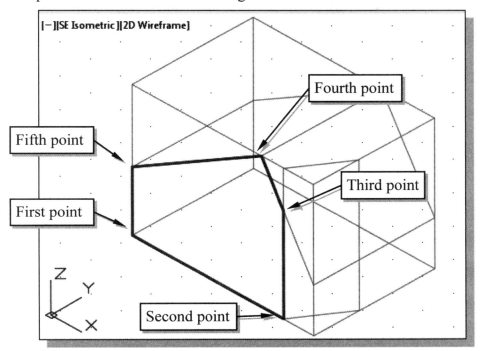

- Note that even though the UCS is aligned to the base plane of the model, the *Object Snap* option enables us to select points on the front plane of the model.

➢ On your own, create three additional lines representing the edges of the inclined face of the design as shown.

Multiple Viewports

1. In the *Menu Bar*, select:

   **[View] → [Viewports] →
   [4 Viewports]**

   ➢ AutoCAD allows us to display different VIEWS of the model simultaneously. Only one viewport is activated at one time. The viewport with the darker border is the active viewport. Move the cursor inside each viewport and notice the different cursor-display inside the active viewport.

2. Activate the **top left viewport** by left-clicking once inside the viewport.

3. Select the **Top** view in the *View* toolbar to change the display of the viewport.

4. On your own, repeat the above steps and use the Realtime Zoom command to set and adjust the displays of the viewports as shown below.

➢ Note that the displayed UCS icons at the lower left corner of each viewport correspond to the orientation of the wireframe model in each viewport.

Use the Mirror Command

1. Activate the top left viewport by left-clicking once inside the viewport.

2. *Pre-select* all the objects in the active viewport by using a selection window.

3. Inside the *active viewport*, **right-click** to bring up the pop-up option menu and select the **Quick Select** option.

4. In the *Quick Select* dialog box, select **Layer** from the *Properties* list.

5. Set the *Value* box to **Object**.

6. In the *How to apply* section, confirm the **Include in new selection set** option is selected.

7. Switch *OFF* the **Append to current selection set**.

8. Click on the **OK** button to accept the settings.

•   AutoCAD will now **filter out** objects that are not on layer *Object*.

9. Click on the **Mirror** icon in the *Modify* toolbar.

10. Inside the graphics window, hold down the **[SHIFT]** key and **right-click** once to bring up the *Object Snap* shortcut menu.

11. Select the **Midpoint** option in the pop-up window.

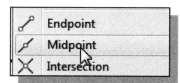

12. Inside the active viewport, click on the left vertical line of the wireframe model. With the *Midpoint* snap option, the midpoint of the line is selected.

13. Move the cursor toward the right vertical line in the active viewport; left-click once when the **Intersection** symbol is displayed as shown.

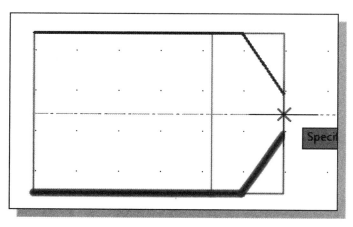

14. In the command prompt area, the message "*Delete Source Objects? [Yes/No] <N>:*" is displayed. Inside the graphics window, right-click once to bring up the option menu and select **No** to keep both sets of objects.

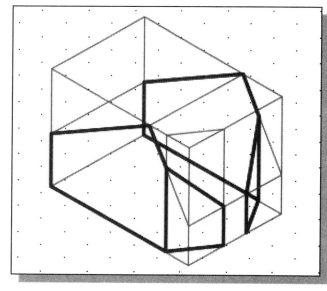

Turn *OFF* the Construction Lines

1. On the *Object Properties* toolbar, choose the ***Layer Control*** box with the left-mouse-button.

2. Move the cursor over the **light-bulb** icon for layer *Construction*, **left-click once**, and notice the icon color is changed to a gray tone color, representing the layer (layer *Construction*) is turned *OFF*.

3. In the *Menu Bar*, select:

   [View] → [Viewports] → [1 Viewport]

   • Viewports can also be used as a way of checking the integrity of the constructed 3D models. Feel free to switch to multiple viewports in the following sections of this tutorial.

4. On your own, create the additional **object lines** connecting the two sets of objects as shown below.

➤ The V-cut feature of the design is the last feature, and perhaps the most difficult one, to create in the CAD system. Based on your knowledge of modeling with AutoCAD, how would you create this feature? What are the more difficult aspects of creating this feature?

Create a New UCS

➤ Besides using the preset UCS planes, AutoCAD also allows us to change our viewpoint and create new UCS planes. We will create a UCS plane aligning to the inclined plane of the design.

1. In the *Menu Bar*, select:
   [Tools] → [New UCS] → [3 Point].

• Note that other options are also available to aid in the creation of new UCS planes.

2. In the command prompt area, the message "*Specify New Origin point <0,0,0>:*" is displayed. Pick the lower-left corner of the inclined plane as shown.

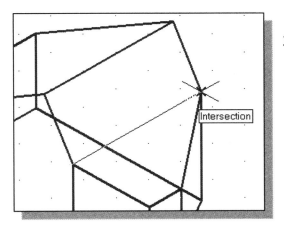

3. In the command prompt area, the message "*Specify point on positive portion of X-axis:*" is displayed. Pick the lower right corner of the inclined plane as shown.

4. In the command prompt area, the message "*Specify point on positive portion of X-axis:*" is displayed. Pick the top left corner of the inclined plane as shown.

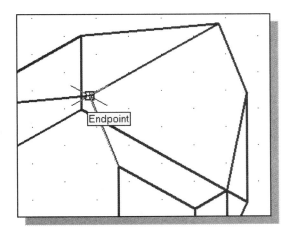

5. In the *Menu Bar*, select

   **[View] → [Display] →
   [UCS Icon] → [Properties]**

6. In the *UCS Icon* window, switch the *UCS icon style* to **2D** as shown.

7. Click on the **OK** button to accept the settings.

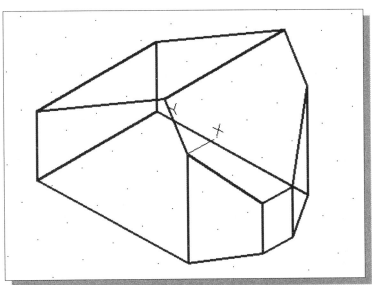

Create a New Named View

- Besides using the preset views, AutoCAD also allows us to change our viewpoint and create new views, which can be saved and restored by name for convenient access. We will create a new view aligned to the new UCS plane we just created.

    1. In the *Menu Bar*, select
       [View] → [3D Views] → [Plan View] → [Current UCS].

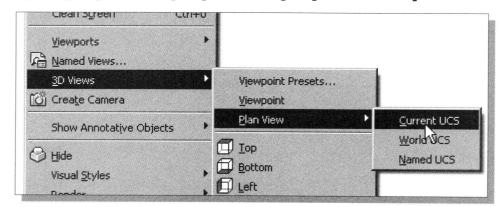

- The graphics window is now adjusted to display the current UCS plane.

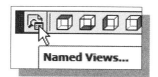

2. Click on the **Named Views** icon in the *View* toolbar.

3. In the *View* dialog box, click on the **New** button to create a new named view.

4. In the *New View* dialog box, enter **Auxiliary** as the new *View name* and confirm the **Current display** option and the **Save layer Snapshot with view** option are switched *ON* and the *UCS option* is set to **Unnamed**.

5. Click on the **OK** button to accept the settings and create the named view.

6. In the *View* dialog box, the new named view (Auxiliary) is added to the *Named Views* list. Note that we can always switch to this view by using the **Set Current** option.

7. Click on the **OK** button to accept the settings.

8. In the *View* toolbar, select **SE Isometric View**.

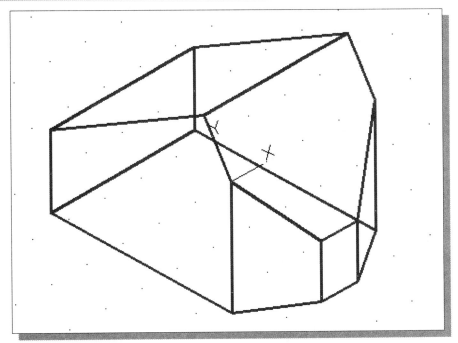

Create the V-Cut Feature on the Inclined Plane

1. On your own, create two lines that are **0.2″** away from the top corners of the model, which are also rotated **45 degrees** relative to the top edge of the model.

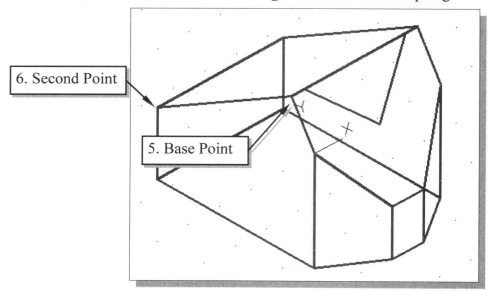

2. Click on the **Copy Object** icon in the *Modify* toolbar.

3. In the command prompt area, the message "*Select objects:*" is displayed. Pick the two inclined lines we just created.

4. Inside the graphics window, **right-click** once to accept the selections.

5. In the command prompt area, the message "*Specify base point or displacement, or [Multiple]:*" is displayed. Pick the **top left corner** as the base point to create the copy.

6. In the command prompt area, the message "*Specify second point of displacement or <use first point as displacement>:*" is displayed. Pick the corresponding corner on the **backside** of the model as shown in the above figure.

7. On your own, create addition lines to define the edges of the V-cut and use the **Trim** command to complete the model as shown.

8. Click on the **Front View** icon in the *View* toolbar.

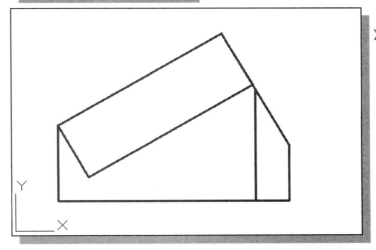

➢ Note that the V-cut we created, using the Copy command, does not represent a cut that passes through the entire block.

Extend the Cut and GRIP Editing

1. Select the **Extend** command icon in the *Modify* toolbar.

2. In the command prompt area, the message "*Select boundary edges... Select objects:*" is displayed. Pick the left vertical line as the *boundary edge*.

3. Inside the graphics window, **right-click** to accept the selection.

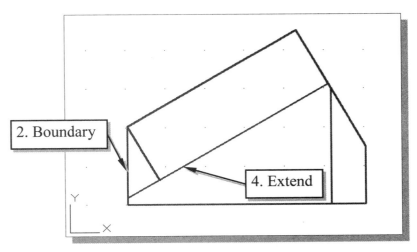

4. The message "*Select object to Extend or [Project/ Edge/ Undo]:*" is displayed in the command prompt area. Pick the bottom edge of the V-cut to extend.

5. Inside the graphics window, **right-click** to activate the option menu and select **Enter** with the left-mouse-button to end the Extend command.

6. Click on the **SW Isometric View** icon to reset the display to the preset isometric view.

7. *Pre-select* the top edge of the *V-block* as shown.

8. Left-click once on the lower right grip point on the selected line.

•   Selecting the grip points located at the end of the line or arc allows us to **STRETCH** the selected line.

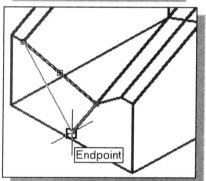

9. Move the cursor toward and select the lower corner of the V-cut as shown.

➢   On your own, repeat the above steps and use the grip editing options and complete the wireframe model as shown below.

Review Questions:

1. List and describe three different types of 3D computer geometric modeling software available today.

2. What is a *Named View*?

3. What is the difference between **Stretch** and **Extend**?

4. List and describe the methods available in AutoCAD to create a new UCS plane.

5. What is the difference between **Copy** and **Mirror** in AutoCAD?

6. Identify and describe the following commands:

a)

b)

c)

d)

Exercises: (Unless otherwise specified, dimensions are in inches.)

1.

2.

3.

4.

5.

Chapter 5
3D Surface Modeling

Learning Objectives

- ♦ **Create 3D Surface Models**
- ♦ **Understand and Apply the Different Surface Modeling Techniques**
- ♦ **Understand the Use of the 2D SOLID Command**
- ♦ **Understand the Use of 3D FACE Command**
- ♦ **Use the Hidden Edge Option**

Introduction

As illustrated in the previous chapters, there are no surfaces in a wireframe model; it consists only of points, lines, and curves that describe the edges of the object. Surface modeling was developed to provide the surface information that is missing in wireframe modeling. Essentially, defining the skin of a design creates a surface model. Although it is possible to create a surface model without using a wireframe model, in most cases it is much easier to create a surface model on top of a wireframe model. In surface modeling, a wireframe model can be used to provide information about the edges and corners so that the desired faces can be easily positioned and placed.

Surface modeling is more sophisticated than wireframe modeling in that surface modelers define not only the edges of 3D objects, but also the surfaces. Surface modeling provides hiding, shading, and rendering capabilities that are not available in wireframe modeling. Surface models do not provide the physical properties that solid models provide, such as mass, weight, center of gravity, and so on.

The AutoCAD surface modeler defines faceted surfaces using a filled polygon. The created faces of surface models are only planar, which means the surface models can only have approximate curved surfaces. It is important to note that the AutoCAD surface modeler does not create true curved surfaces. To differentiate these two types of surfaces, faceted surfaces are called **meshes** in AutoCAD. Because of the use of faceted approximation on true curved surfaces, the computer requirements of most faceted surface modelers are typically much less than that of solid modelers. Faceted surface modeling usually provides reasonably good representations of 3D designs with fast rendering and shading capabilities. Faceted surface models are also useful for creating geometry with unusual surface patterns, such as a 3D topographical model of mountainous terrain.

AutoCAD 2017 provides three basic methods for creating surfaces – the **2D Solid**, **3D Face** and **Region** commands. The three commands were developed parallel to the historical development of the different types of computer modelers.

- **2D Solid**: The first generation surface command available in AutoCAD. Used mostly to fill an area in the sketch plane of the current UCS. This type of surface is not a true 3D surface.

- **3D Face**: Creates a true 3D planar surface (allowing X, Y and Z coordinates) of three-sided or four-sided shapes. This is the type of surface developed primarily for creating faceted surface models.

- **Region**: Creates a 2D surface of arbitrary shape from existing 2D entities. This command creates the most flexible and the most complicated type of surface available in AutoCAD. This command was developed to allow manipulation of 2D surfaces using one of the solid modeling construction techniques, namely, the **Constructive Solid Geometry** method.

Although all three commands can be used to create planar surfaces, the resulting surfaces are not equal. In fact, the three commands are developed with specific tasks in mind. The **2D Solid** command is mostly used in 2D drawings to create 2D filled area and the **Region** command is designed so that general 2D shapes can be easily transformed into solid models. The **3D Face** command is the only one that is designed specifically for surface modeling and therefore it is the most suitable for such tasks. The use of the **2D Solid** and **Region** commands in 3D surface modeling can be somewhat awkward and at times very difficult. Note that the use of the **Region** command will be focused on in the solid modeling chapters of this text.

As one can imagine, sketching each surface manually can be very time consuming and tedious. AutoCAD also provides additional tools for more advanced surface modeling, such as **Tabulated surfaces**, **Ruled surfaces** and **Revolved surfaces**. These tools are basically automated procedures, which can be used to define and create multiple copies of planar surfaces in specific directions. The principles and concepts used by these tools are also used in creating solid models, which are covered in chapter six through chapter eight of this text. You are encouraged to re-examine these commands after you have finished the solid modeling chapters.

In this chapter, the general procedures to create surface models are illustrated. The use of the **2D Solid** and **3D Face** commands are illustrated and differences discussed. We will also demonstrate the use of the more advanced surface modeling tools. Two wireframe models, which were created in the previous chapters, will be converted into surface models.

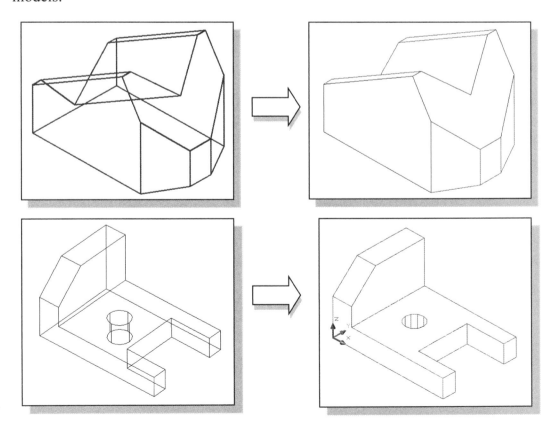

Starting Up AutoCAD 2017

1. Select the **AutoCAD 2017** option on the *Program* menu or select the **AutoCAD 2017** icon on the *Desktop*.

2. In the *AutoCAD Today Startup* dialog box, select the **Open a Drawing** icon with a single click of the left-mouse-button.

3. Click on the ***V-block.dwg*** filename to open the *V-block* wireframe model that was created in the previous chapter. (Use the Browse option to locate the file if it is not displayed.)

- The *V-block* wireframe model is retrieved and displayed in the graphics window.

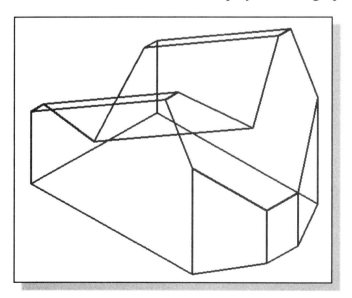

The UCS Toolbar and the Meshes Commands

1. In the *Menu Bar,* select **[Tools]** → **[Toolbars]** → **[AutoCAD]**.

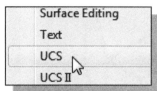

2. Select **UCS**, with the left-mouse-button, to display the *UCS* toolbar on the screen.

➤ The options available in the *UCS* toolbar allow us to quickly orient and align the UCS.

3. Click on the **Mesh** tab to show the mesh commands available in AutoCAD.

•   Note that a variety of 2D mesh modeling commands are available to create meshes. On your own, move the cursor on top of the different commands and read the brief description of the commands.

Create a Mesh Surface Using the 2D Solid Command

➤ The first generation surface command available in AutoCAD was the **2D Solid** command. In AutoCAD 2017, this command can only be accessed through the command prompt area, which is an indication that this command is slowly being phased out. The 2D Solid command is used to fill an area in the sketch plane of the current UCS. It is therefore necessary to properly orient the UCS prior to using the **2D Solid** command.

1. Select the **3 Point UCS** icon in the *UCS* toolbar.

•   The **3 Point UCS** option allows us to specify the new X-axis and Y-axis directions to align the UCS.

2. In the command prompt area, the message *"Specify new origin point<0,0,0>:"* is displayed. Pick the **lower right corner** of the front face of the wireframe model as shown.

3. In the command prompt area, the message "*Specify point on positive portion of X-axis:*" is displayed. Pick the adjacent corner toward the right side of the model as shown.

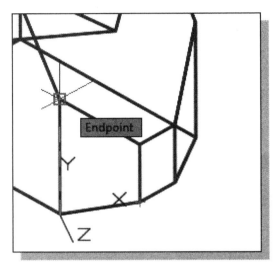

4. In the command prompt area, the message "*Specify point on positive portion of X-axis:*" is displayed. Pick the right corner of the inclined plane as shown.

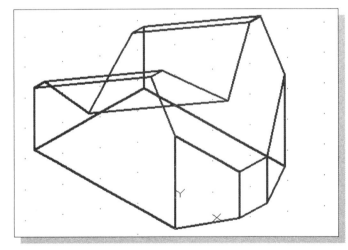

-   The new UCS is aligned to the vertical inclined plane as shown.

5. In the *command prompt area*, enter **Solid** to activate the 2D Solid command.

6. Place the first corner point of the 2D solid at the origin of the new UCS.

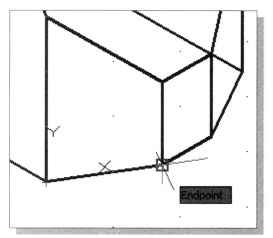

7. In the command prompt area, the message "*Specify second point:*" is displayed. Pick the bottom right corner of the inclined plane as shown.

8. In the command prompt area, the message "*Specify third point:*" is displayed. Pick the corner directly above the origin of the UCS as shown.

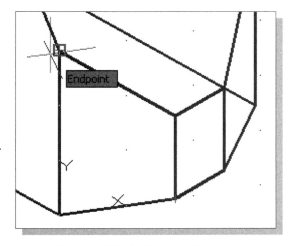

- The **2D Solid** command requires the third point to be specified *diagonally opposite* to the second point. This seemingly strange way of specifying the third corner was established when the **2D Solid** command was first introduced back in the mid-1980s. Note that the **3D Face** command, the second-generation surface command in AutoCAD, does not follow this convention.

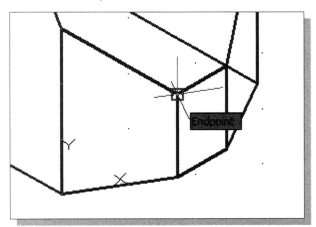

9. In the command prompt area, the message "*Specify fourth point or [Exit]:*" is displayed. Pick the corner directly above the second point we selected as shown in the figure.

10. Inside the graphics window, **right-click once** to end the **2D Solid** command.

➢ The **2D Solid** command allows the creation of *three-sided* or *four-sided* filled polygons, which can be used to represent faces of surface models. Note that in the above steps, we could accept the three-sided polygon after defining the third corner.

Using the Visual Styles Toolbar

1. Move the cursor to the *Visualize* toolbar panel and **left-click** on the downward triangle to display a list of available options.

❖ Note that ten different *Visual Styles* are available; descriptions of the six more commonly used styles are as follows:

- **2D Wireframe**: Displays the objects using lines and curves to represent the boundaries of objects created. Linetypes and lineweights are visible with this option. Note that this is the default AutoCAD display mode.

- **Conceptual Visual Style**: Creates a shaded image of polygon faces and solids that uses the Gooch face style, a transition between cool and warm colors rather than dark to light. The effect is less realistic, but it can make the details of the model easier to see.

- **Hidden**: Displays the objects using the 3D wireframe representation with lines that are located behind surfaces and solids removed.

- **Realistic Visual Style**: Creates a Gouraud-shaded image of polygon faces and solids that gives the objects a smooth and realistic appearance.

- **Shaded Style**: Shades the objects between the polygon faces. The objects appear flatter and less smooth than Gouraud-shaded objects.

- **3D Wireframe**: Displays the objects using lines and curves to represent the boundaries of objects created. Displays a shaded 3D user coordinate system (UCS) icon. Note that linetypes and lineweights are not visible with this option.

2. Click on the **Realistic Visual Style** icon to display the shaded image of the model.

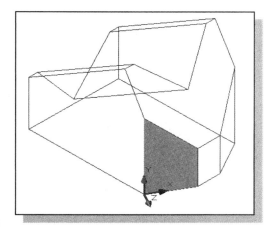

❖ Only one surface exists in our model. The surface was created with the **2D Solid** command.

3. Select **Free Orbit** in the *View* pull-down menu as shown.

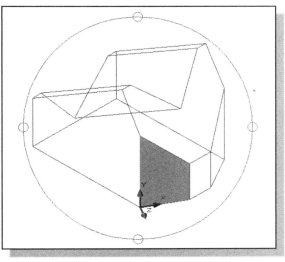

4. Inside the *arcball*, press down the left-mouse-button and drag it to rotate the model freely in 3D space. Observe the display of the shaded surface in contrast to the 3D wireframe edges that are located behind it.

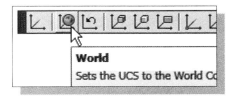

5. In the *UCS* toolbar, select the **World UCS**. This option resets the UCS to align to the world coordinate system.

6. On your own, reset the display to the **SE Isometric View** before continuing to the next section.

Create a Mesh Surface Using the 3D Face Command

- The second generation of surface command made available in AutoCAD was the **3D Face** command. The **3D Face** command can be used to create true 3D planar surfaces by allowing the X, Y and Z coordinates of the corners to be selected independently of the current UCS. The created polygon can be a three-sided or four-sided shape. This command is the primary construction tool for surface modeling in AutoCAD.

1. In the *Menu Bar*, select **[Draw]** → **[Modeling]** → **[Meshes]** → **[3D Face]**.

2. In the *command prompt area*, the message "_3dface Specify first point or [invisible]:" is displayed. Pick the lower right corner of the vertical inclined face of the model as shown.

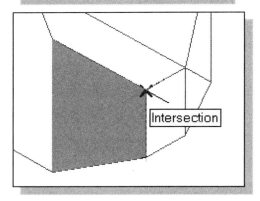

3. In the *command prompt area*, the message "Specify second point or [invisible]:" is displayed. Pick the adjacent corner above the previous selected corner of the vertical inclined face as shown.

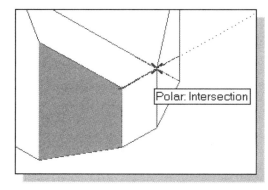

4. In the *command prompt area*, the message "Specify third point or [invisible]:" is displayed. Pick the adjacent corner of the right vertical face of the model as shown.

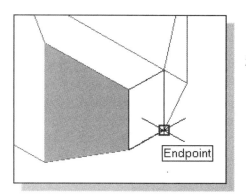

5. In the command prompt area, the message "*Specify fourth point or [invisible] <Create three-sided face>:*" is displayed. Pick the corner below the last selected corner as shown.

6. In the command prompt area, the message "*Specify third point or [invisible] <exit>:*" is displayed. Pick the back corner of the model as shown.

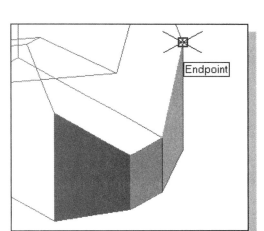

7. In the command prompt area, the message "*Specify fourth point or [invisible] <Create three-sided face>:*" is displayed. Pick the back corner of the model as shown.

• Note that this surface is created independent of the UCS and two corners of the previous face were used to position this face.

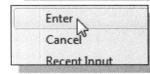

8. Inside the graphics window, right-click to activate the option menu and select **Enter** with the left-mouse-button to end the 3D Face command.

The ViewCube

The ViewCube is a 3D navigation tool that appears when the 3D graphics system is enabled. With the ViewCube, you can switch between standard and isometric views.

Once the ViewCube is displayed, it is shown in one of the corners of the graphics window over the model in an inactive state. The ViewCube also provides visual feedback about the current viewpoint of the model as view changes occur. When the cursor is positioned over the ViewCube, it becomes active and allows you to switch to one of the available preset views, roll the current view, or change to the Home view of the model.

1. Move the cursor over the ViewCube and notice the different sides of the ViewCube become highlighted and can be activated.

2. Single left-click when the Front side is activated as shown. The current view is set to viewing the Front side.

3. Move the cursor over the **counterclockwise** arrow of the ViewCube and notice the **Orbit** option becomes highlighted.

4. Single left-click to activate the **counterclockwise** option as shown. The current view is orbited 90 degrees; we are still viewing the Front side.

5. Move the cursor over the **Left** arrow of the ViewCube and notice the **Orbit** option becomes highlighted.

6. Single left-click to activate the **Left** arrow option as shown. The current view is now set to viewing the Top side.

7. Move the cursor over the **top edge** of the ViewCube and notice the roll option becomes highlighted.

8. Single left-click to activate the **Roll** option as shown. The view will be adjusted to roll 45 degrees.

9. Move the cursor over the ViewCube and drag with the left-mouse-button to activate the **Free Rotation** option.

➢ The orientation of the model can also be changed to base on either the UCS or the WCS by clicking on the coordinate setting option below the ViewCube as shown.

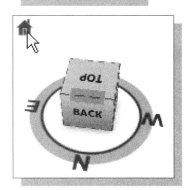

10. Move the cursor over the **Home** icon of the ViewCube and notice the **Home View** option becomes highlighted.

11. Single left-click to activate the **Home View** option as shown. The view will be adjusted back to the default **SW Isometric** view.

12. In the *Visual Style Controls* list, click on the **2D Wireframe → Hidden** icon to display the model with hidden lines removed.

• The *Quick Display* controls list, located near the upper left corner of the graphics area, provides quick access to many display-related commands.

13. On your own, use the **ViewCube** to rotate the model and examine the constructed surface model.

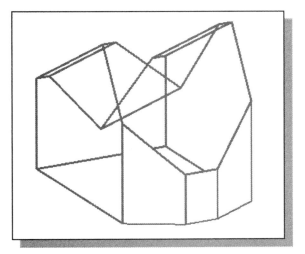

Create a Surface of Irregular Shape

- The **3D Face** command allows us to create three-sided or four-sided polygons. For surfaces of irregular shape, the Invisible Edge option is available in conjunction with the 3D Face command. Note that the Invisible Edge option cannot be applied to polygons created by the 2D Solid command.

1. Select the **2D Wireframe** in the *Visual Styles* toolbar.

- The 2D Wireframe command resets the display to the default AutoCAD display mode. Note that this step is required for the Invisible Edge option to work correctly.

2. In the *command prompt area*, enter **3dface** to activate the command as shown.

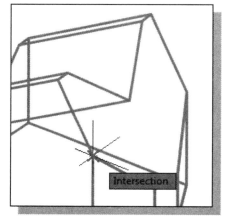

3. In the *command prompt area*, the message "*_3dface Specify first point or [invisible]:*" is displayed. Pick the right corner of the model as shown.

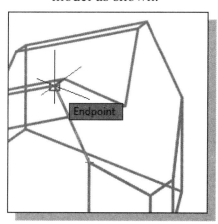

4. In the *command prompt area*, the message "*Specify second point or [invisible]:*" is displayed. Pick the top front corner of the model as shown.

5. In the *command prompt area*, the message "*Specify third point or [invisible] <exit>:*" is displayed. Pick the top corner of the model adjacent to the previously selected corner as shown.

6. In the command prompt area, the message "*Specify fourth point or [invisible] <Create three-sided face>:*" is displayed. Pick the corner below the last selected corner as shown.

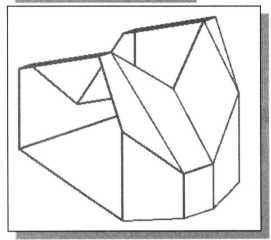

7. On your own, repeat the zigzagging pattern to define polygons until all corners of the inclined surface have been selected and additional polygons are created as shown in the figure. Note that the last polygon we created is a three-sided polygon.

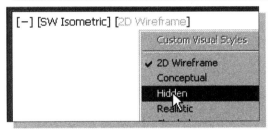

8. In the *Visual Styles* toolbar, click on the **Hidden** icon to display the model with hidden lines removed. Note that the edges of the polygons are displayed as shown.

9. On your own, examine the model by selecting the different *Visual Styles*.

10. Rest the *Visual Styles* toolbar to **2D Wireframe**, the default AutoCAD display mode.

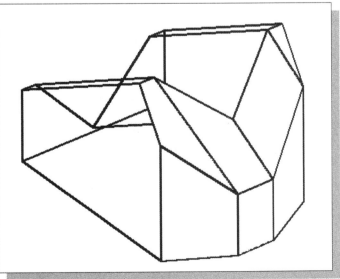

Use the Invisible Edge Option

- The Invisible Edge option is used to turn off the display of selected edges and therefore allow the adjacent polygons, created by the 3D Face command, to appear as being joined together. (Note the operation must be done in the **2D Wireframe** mode.)

1. In the command prompt area, enter **Edge** to activate the command as shown.

2. In the command prompt area, the message "*Specify edge of 3dface to toggle visibility or [Display]:*" is displayed. Pick **the three edges** inside the inclined surface as shown.

3. Inside the graphics window, right-click to activate the option menu and select **Enter** to end the Edge command.

4. Set the *Visual Style* toolbar to **Hidden**.

5. On your own, examine the model by selecting the different *Visual Styles*.

- The selected edges are removed from the display so that the face of the inclined surface of the model appears to be more realistic.

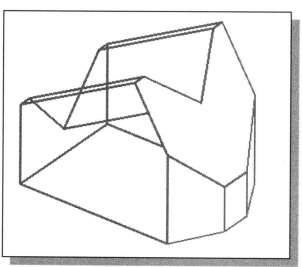

Repositioning with the Grip Editing Tools

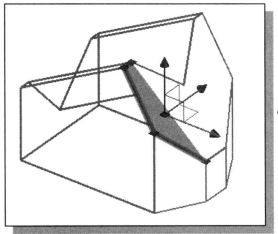

1. Select one of the 3D faces we created by clicking on the front edge of the inclined surface as shown.

   • Four grip points, the small rectangles displayed at the corners of the highlighted polygon, can be used to adjust the size and shape of the highlighted polygon.

2. Move the cursor on one of the grip points. Notice the grip editing axes are automatically aligned to the grip point.

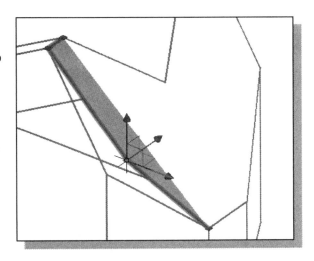

3. Click on one of the axes and drag with the left-mouse-button to move the grip point. (Clicking on the axis constrains the movement to the selected axis.)

4. Press the **[Esc]** key to deselect the highlighted entities.

➢ On your own, repeat the above steps and complete the surface model of the design.

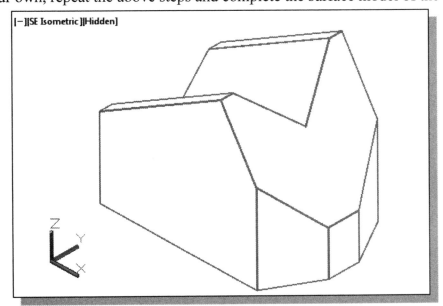

The *Locator* Wireframe Model

1. Click on the **Open** icon in the *Standard* toolbar.

2. In the *Select File* window, pick the **Locator** file that was created in Chapter 3.

3. Click **Open** to open the model file.

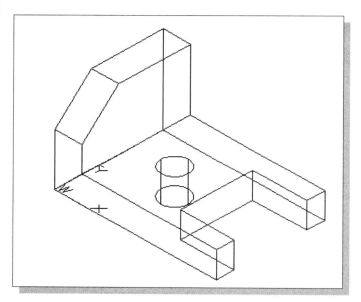

Moving Objects to a Different Layer

❖ Prior to creating additional surfaces, we will first organize the existing geometry that has been constructed.

1. Click **Layers Properties Manager** in the *Layers* toolbar.

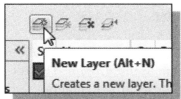

2. Click on the **New** button to create new layers.

3. Create **three new layers** with the following settings:

Layer	Color	Linetype	Lineweight
Construction	White	Continuous	Default
Wireframe	Blue	Continuous	0.30mm
Surface	Cyan	Continuous	Default

4. Click on the **Close** button to accept the settings and exit the *Layer Properties Manager* dialog box.

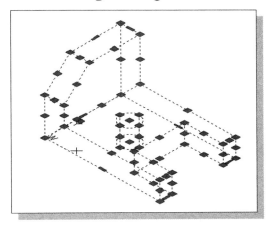

5. Inside the graphics window, pre-select all entities by using the left-mouse-button to create a *selection window* enclosing all entities.

•   Note that all selected entities are highlighted.

6. On the *Object Properties* toolbar, choose the **Layer Control** box with the left-mouse-button.

•   Notice the layer name displayed in the *Layer Control* box is the selected object's assigned layer and layer properties.

7. In the *Layer Control* box, click on the **Wireframe** layer name as shown.

❖ All entities of the *Locator* model are moved to the *Wireframe* layer.

8. Press the [**Esc**] key twice to deselect all highlighted entities.

Advanced Meshed Surface Modeling Commands

❖ Several of the advanced surface-modeling commands are displayed in the *Meshed Surface Modeling* toolbar, which is placed under the **Mesh** tab in the *Ribbon*. These commands allow us to quickly create and duplicate surfaces in specific manners.

- **Revolved Surface**: Creates a surface mesh by rotating a group of objects about an axis.

- **Tabulated Surface**: Creates a surface mesh representing a general tabulated surface defined by a path curve and a direction vector. The resulting mesh is a series of parallel polygons running along a specified path.

- **Ruled Surface**: Creates a surface mesh between two objects.

- **Edge Surface**: Creates a surface patch mesh from four edges.

SurfTab1 & SurfTab2 system variables: These two variables are used to set the number of increments used by the Ruled Surface and Tabulated Surface commands. The default values are set to six, which means any curve will be approximated with six straight lines.

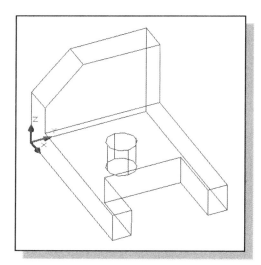

1. On your own, use the **Free Orbit** command and adjust the display of the wireframe model so that the four vertical lines connecting the two circles are visible as shown.

- To illustrate the use of the Ruled Surface and Tabulated Surface commands, we will first split the top circle into two arcs. Note that these surfacing commands allow us to construct a polygon mesh for different situations and regions. The split of the circle is necessary in creating a mapped surface on the top plane of the model.

2. Select **Break** in the *Modify* toolbar under the **Home** tab.

- The Break command can be used to erase parts of objects or split an object in two. Note that we can only erase parts of a circle. We will therefore erase a portion of the circle and then split the circle into two arcs.

3. Select the top circle as shown. Note that the portion defined by two points will be erased.

- By default, AutoCAD treats the selection point as the first break point. We can override the first point by choosing **First point** in the option menu.

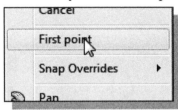

4. In the command prompt area, the message "*Specific second break point or [First point]:*" is displayed. Right-click once and select **First point** in the option menu.

5. In the command prompt area, the message "*Specific first break point:*" is displayed. Choose the top endpoint of the vertical line on the right as shown.

6. In the command prompt area, the message "*Specific second break point:*" is displayed. Choose the top endpoint of the vertical line as shown.

- One quarter of the circle has been erased. We will next split the arc into two arcs, again using the **Break** command.

7. Select **Break** in the *Modify* toolbar.

8. Select the top arc as shown.

• By default, AutoCAD treats the selection point as the first break point. We can override the first point by choosing **First point** in the option menu.

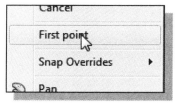

9. In the *command prompt area*, the message "*Specific second break point or [First point]:*" is displayed. Right-click once and select **First point** in the option menu.

10. In the *command prompt area*, the message "*Specific first break point:*" is displayed. Choose the top endpoint of the left vertical line as shown.

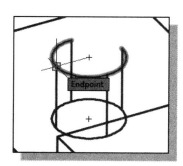

11. In the *command prompt area*, the message "*Specific second break point:*" is displayed. To split an object, choose the **same endpoint** that was previously chosen.

12. Select **Extend** in the *Modify* toolbar. Notice the *Projection* type is set to **View**, as shown in the prompt window.

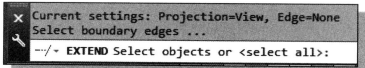

13. Select the right vertical edge to be the extending boundary as shown.

14. Inside the *graphics window*, **right-click** once to accept the selection.

15. Pick the shorter arc near the right endpoint to extend the arc in that direction.

16. Inside the graphics window, right-click once to display the option menu and select **Enter** to end the Extend command.

Use the Tabulated Surface Option

- In AutoCAD, the **TABSURF** command allows us to construct a polygon mesh representing a general tabulated surface defined by a path curve and a direction vector.

1. Set the *Surface* layer as the *Current Layer* by choosing the layer name in the *Layer Control* box as shown.

- We will place the surface model on a different layer than the wireframe model.

2. Click **Tabulated Surface** in the *Primitives* toolbar.

3. In the command prompt area, the message "*Select object for path curve:*" is displayed. Choose the **upper arc** as shown.

4. In the command prompt area, the message "*Select object for direction vector:*" is displayed. Choose the **vertical line** near the top endpoint as shown. Note that the endpoints of the line are used as a reference to determine the direction of the polygon mesh.

5. On your own, use the **Orbit** and **Visual Styles** commands to examine the constructed polygons.

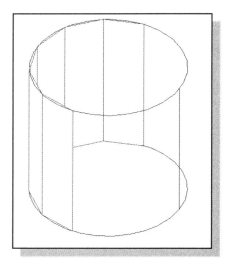

- Exactly six polygons are created and positioned along the selected *path curve*, the upper arc, with the **Tabulated Surface** command. This is set by the *SurfTab1* variable. We can adjust the number of segments to use by typing the word **surftab1** at the command prompt.

❖ Note that a surface modeler using polygons to approximate true curves is called a *faceted surface modeler*.

Use the Ruled Surface Option

- In AutoCAD, the **RULESURF** command allows us to construct a polygon mesh between two objects. We can use two different objects to define the edges of the ruled surface: lines, points, arcs, circles, ellipses, elliptical arcs, polylines, or splines. The two objects to be used as the *rails* of a ruled surface mesh must both be either open or closed. For open curves, AutoCAD starts construction of the ruled surface based on the locations of the specified points on the curves.

1. Pick **Ruled Surface** in the *Draw* pull-down menu.

2. In the command prompt area, the message *"Select first defining curve:"* is displayed. Choose the **lower arc** by clicking on the **right side** as shown.

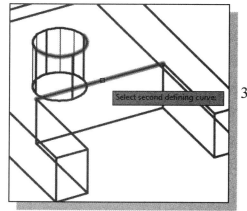

3. In the command prompt area, the message *"Select second defining curve:"* is displayed. Choose the **inside straight edge** on the **right side** as shown.

4. In the *Visual Styles* toolbar, click on the **Hidden** icon to display the model with hidden lines removed.

- The selected edges are removed from the display so that the face of the ruled surface appears to be more realistic.

5. On your own, repeat the above steps and create another ruled surface as shown. (Hint: Use the **Realtime Zoom** function to assist in the selection of the arc.)

6. In the command prompt area, enter **3dface** to activate the **3D Face** command as shown.

- On your own, complete the surface model as shown. (Hint: Use the **Edge** command to hide the edges of the created faces.)

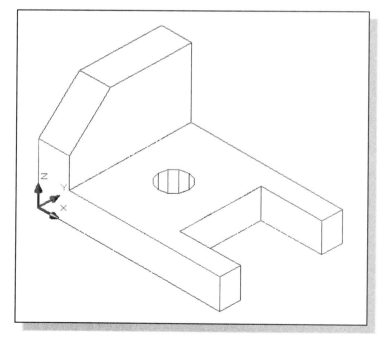

Review Questions:

1. List and describe three differences between *Wireframe models* and *Surface models*.

2. List and describe the three types of surfaces available in AutoCAD.

3. List and describe two different shading options in AutoCAD.

4. What is the difference between the 2D Solid and 3D Face commands in AutoCAD?

5. What is the difference between Tabulated Surface and Ruled Surface in AutoCAD?

6. Identify and describe the following commands:

   a)

   b)

   c)

Exercises: All dimensions are in inches.

1.

2.

3.

4.

5.

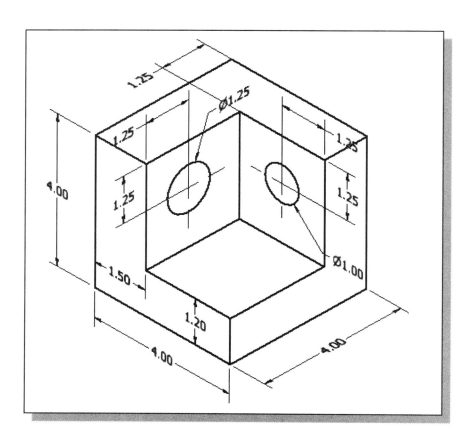

Chapter 6
Solid Modeling – Constructive Solid Geometry

Learning Objectives

- ♦ **Understand the Constructive Solid Geometry Concept**
- ♦ **Create a Binary Tree**
- ♦ **Understand the Basic Boolean Operations**
- ♦ **Create Solids Using AutoCAD Primitive Solids**
- ♦ **Generate Shaded SOLID Images**
- ♦ **Use SteeringWheels**

Introduction

In the previous chapters, we have looked at wireframe modeling and surface modeling. Wireframe modeling describes only the corners and edges of designs. Surface modeling describes part surfaces but not interiors. Although surface models are fairly good representations of the actual designs, designers are still required to interactively examine surface models to ensure that the various surfaces on a model are contiguous throughout. Many of the concepts used in 3D wireframe and surface modelers are incorporated in the solid modeling scheme, but it is solid modeling that offers the most advantages as a design tool.

In the solid modeling presentation scheme, the solid definitions include nodes, edges, and surfaces, and it is a complete and unambiguous mathematical representation of a precisely enclosed and filled volume. Two predominant methods for representing solid models are **constructive solid geometry** (CSG) representation and **boundary representation** (B-rep). CSG defines a model in terms of combining basic solid shapes and B-rep defines a model in terms of its edges and surfaces. AutoCAD's solid modeler is a hybrid modeler; the user interface and construction techniques are CSG-based, whereas the B-rep capabilities are invoked automatically and are transparent to the user.

In this chapter, we will discuss the fundamental concepts of solid modeling. We will demonstrate the procedure required to construct a solid model using AutoCAD's CSG-based user interface.

The *Guide-Block* Design

Constructive Solid Geometry Concept

In the 1980s, one of the main advancements in **Solid Modeling** was the development of the **Constructive Solid Geometry** (CSG) method. CSG describes the solid model as the combination of basic three-dimensional shapes (**primitive solids**). The basic primitive solid set typically includes Rectangular-prism (Block), Cylinder, Cone, Sphere, and Torus (Donut). Two solid objects can be combined into one object in various ways; these operations are known as **Boolean operations**. There are three basic Boolean operations: **UNION (Join)**, **SUBTRACT (Cut)**, and **INTERSECT**. The UNION operation combines the two volumes included in the different solids into a single solid. The SUBTRACT operation subtracts the volume of one solid object from the other solid object. The INTERSECT operation keeps only the volume common to both solid objects. The CSG method is also known as the **Machinist's Approach**, as the method is parallel to machine shop practices.

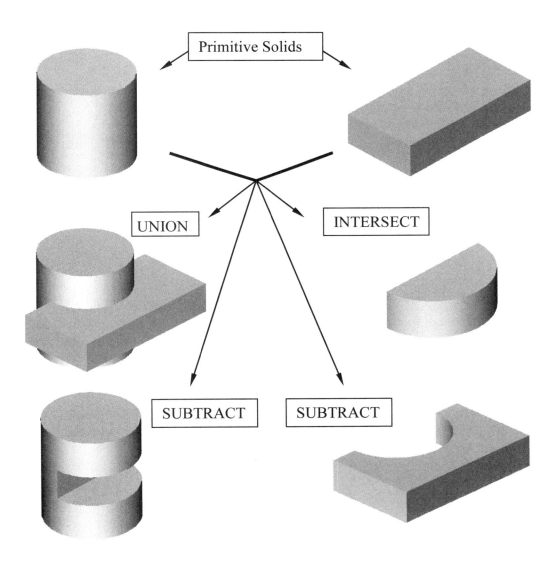

Binary Tree

CSG is also referred to as the method used to store a solid model in the database. The resulting solid can be easily represented by what is called a **binary tree**. In a binary tree, the terminal branches (leaves) are the various primitives that are linked together to make the final solid object (the root). The binary tree is an effective way to represent the steps required to construct the solid model. Complicated solid models can be modeled by considering the different combinations of Boolean operations required in the binary tree. This provides a convenient and intuitive way of modeling that imitates the manufacturing process. A binary tree is an effective way to plan your modeling strategy before you start creating anything.

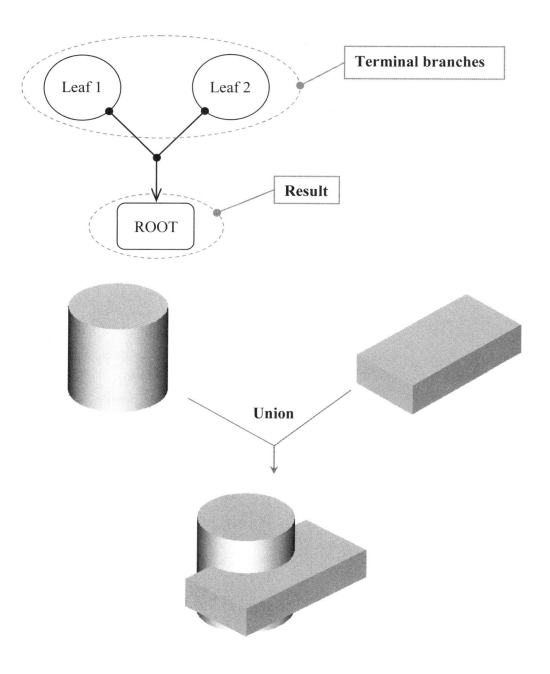

The *Guide-Block* CSG Binary Tree

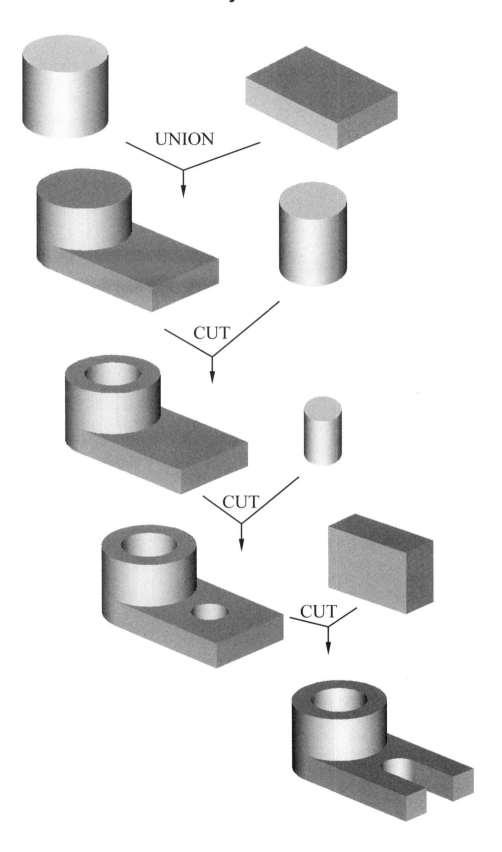

Starting Up AutoCAD 2017

1. Select the **AutoCAD 2017** option on the *Program* menu or select the **AutoCAD 2017** icon on the *Desktop*.

2. In the *Startup* dialog box, select the **Start from Scratch** option with a single click of the left-mouse-button.

3. In the *Default Settings* section, pick **Metric** as the drawing units.

4. Click **OK** to accept the settings and exit the *Startup* window.

Layers Setup

1. In the *Menu Bar,* select **[Tools]** → **[Toolbars]** → **[AutoCAD]** → **[Layers]**.

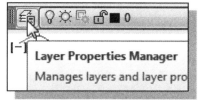

2. Click **Layers Properties Manager** in the *Layers* toolbar.

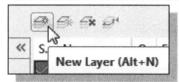

3. Click on the **New** button. Notice a layer is automatically added to the list of layers.

4. Create a **new layer** with the following settings:

Layer	*Color*	*Linetype*
Solid_Objects	**Cyan**	**Continuous**

5. Set layer ***Solid_Objects*** as the *Current Layer*.

6. Click on the **Close** button to accept the settings and exit the *Layer Properties Manager* dialog box.

Create the First 3D Object

1. Click on the down arrow below the first icon of the 3D Modeling toolbar as shown.

❖ Note that the first icon of the *3DModeling* toolbar contains the basic set of pre-defined solids, primitive solids, available in **AutoCAD® 2017**.

2. On your own, move the cursor on top of the different icons and examine the available options.

➤ Also note that the typical basic primitive solid set includes **Box (Rectangular-prism)**, **Cylinder**, **Cone**, **Sphere**, and **Torus** (Donut).

- We will first create a **75 × 50 × 15** rectangular block.

3. In the *Modeling* toolbar, click on the **Box** icon. In the command prompt area, the message "*Specify corner of box or [Center] <0,0,0>:*" is displayed.

4. Pick a location that is near the lower left corner of the graphics window.

5. In the command prompt area, the message "*Specify corner or [Cube/Length]:*" is displayed. Enter **@75,50 [ENTER]**.

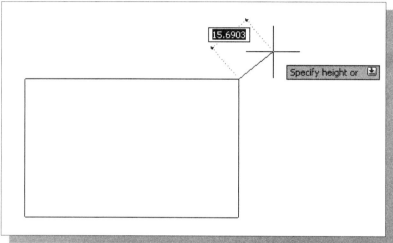

6. In the command prompt area, the message "*Specify Height:*" is displayed. Enter **15 [ENTER]**.

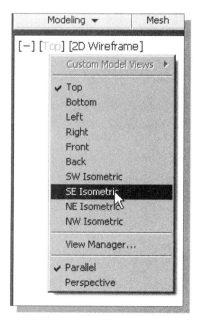

7. In the *View Display Controls* list, click on the **SE Isometric View** icon to set the display of the solid model.

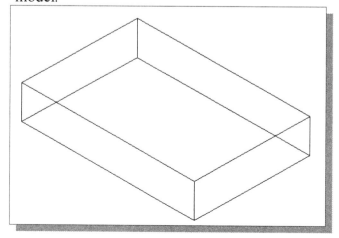

Create the Second Solid Feature

- We will next create a cylinder block as the second solid feature.

1. In the *3D Modeling* toolbar, click on the **Cylinder** icon. In the command prompt area, the message "*Specify center point for base cylinder or [Elliptical] <0,0,0>:*" is displayed.

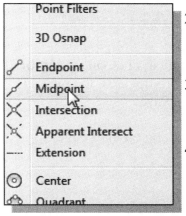

2. Inside the graphics window, press down the [**SHIFT**] key and **right-mouse-click** once to bring up the *Object Snap* shortcut menu.

3. Select the **Midpoint** option in the shortcut menu. Snap to and select the midpoint of the bottom-left edge of the rectangular block as shown in the figure below.

4. In the command prompt area, the message "*Specify radius for base of cylinder or [Diameter]:*" is displayed. Snap to and select one of the **endpoints** of the bottom edge of the rectangular block.

5. In the command prompt area, the message "*Specify height of cylinder or [Center of other end]:*" is displayed. Move the cursor up to set the height direction and enter **40 [ENTER]**.

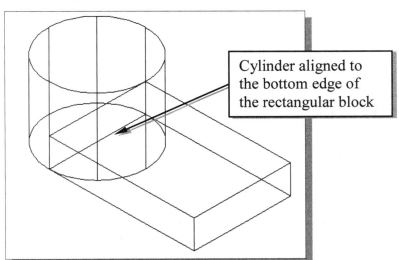

Cylinder aligned to the bottom edge of the rectangular block

- We have created **two solid objects**, one rectangular box and one cylinder, that are displayed on the screen.

Boolean Operation – *UNION*

1. Move the cursor on top of the third group of icons, the *Solid Editing* toolbar, which contains the basic set of Boolean operation icons. On your own, read the brief description of each of the Boolean commands.

2. In the *Solid Editing* toolbar, click on the **Union** icon. In the command prompt area, the message "*Select Objects:*" is displayed.

3. Pick both solids by clicking on their edges.

4. Inside the *graphics window*, **right-mouse-click** to accept the selection and proceed with the Union command.

Create the Second Cylinder Feature

- We will create another cylinder as the next solid feature.

1. In the *Modeling* toolbar, click on the **Cylinder** icon. In the command prompt area, the message "*Specify center point for base cylinder or [Elliptical] <0,0,0>:*" is displayed.

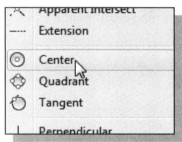

2. Inside the graphics window, press down the **[SHIFT]** key and **right-mouse-click** once to bring up the *Object Snap* shortcut menu.

3. Select the **Center** option in the shortcut menu.

4. Snap to and select the **center of the circle** that is at the **top** of the solid block.

5. In the command prompt area, the message "*Specify radius for base of cylinder or [Diameter]:*" is displayed. Enter 15 as the radius value: **15** [**ENTER**].

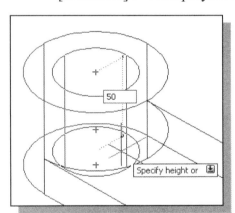

6. In the command prompt area, the message "*Specify radius for base of cylinder or [Diameter]:*" is displayed. Set the extrusion to the downward direction by entering the depth value: **50** [**ENTER**].

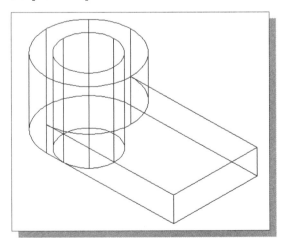

- Two solid objects, the base block and a cylinder, are displayed on the screen. On your own, use the available Views options to confirm the top of the two solids are aligned.

Boolean Operation – *SUBTRACT*

1. In the *Modeling* toolbar, click on the **Subtract** icon. In the command prompt area, the message "*_subtract Select solids and regions to subtract from ... Select Objects:*" is displayed.

2. Pick the **base block** solid by clicking on one of the straight edges.

3. Inside the graphics window, **right-mouse-click** to accept the selection and proceed with the Subtract command.

4. In the command prompt area, the message "*Select solids and regions to subtract... Select Objects:*" is displayed.

5. Pick the cylinder block by clicking on one of the circular edges.

6. Inside the graphics window, **right-mouse-click** to accept the selection and proceed with the Subtract command.

Create another Solid Feature

- As can be seen, the CSG construction approach is quite straightforward. The main task is in positioning and aligning the solid blocks prior to applying a Boolean operation.

1. In the *Modeling* toolbar, click on the **Cylinder** icon. In the command prompt area, the message *"Specify center point for base cylinder or [Elliptical] <0,0,0>:"* is displayed.

2. Inside the graphics window, press down the [**SHIFT**] key and **right-mouse-click** once to bring up the *Object Snap* shortcut menu.

3. Select the **From** option in the shortcut menu.

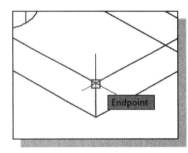

4. Snap to the **top front** corner of the base block and enter **@-30,25** [**ENTER**].

5. In the command prompt area, the message *"Specify radius for base of cylinder or [Diameter]:"* is displayed. Enter **10** [**ENTER**].

6. Move the cursor **downward** and create a cylinder that is longer than the height of the horizontal base as shown.

7. On your own, perform the Boolean **Subtract** operation.

Visual Styles Options

1. Move the cursor to the ***Visualize*** toolbar panel and **left-click** on the downward triangle to display a list of available options.

2. In the *Visual Styles* toolbar, click on the **Conceptual Visual Style** icon to display the shaded image of the solid model. A solid model contains both surfaces and volume.

➢ On your own, examine the solid model by using the **ViewCube**.

Create the Final Feature

- We will create a rectangular cut as the final solid feature of the part. In the previous sections, with some careful planning, we positioned the solid blocks at the correct space locations while we were creating the solids. It is also possible to take a more general approach to orient and position solid blocks in space coordinates.

1. In the *Modeling* toolbar, click on the **Box** icon. In the command prompt area, the message "*Specify corner of box or [Center] <0,0,0>:*" is displayed.

2. In the *Status bar* area, turn off the **Dynamic UCS** option (or hit the [**F6**] key once).

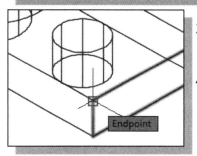

3. Snap to and select the **top front corner** of the base block.

4. In the *command prompt area*, the message "*Specify corner or [Cube/Length]:*" is displayed. Enter **@-30,30** [**ENTER**].

5. In the command prompt area, the message "*Specify height:*" is displayed. For the depth value Enter **20** [**ENTER**].

> Two overlapping solids appear on the screen. We will use the *editing tools* to orient the cutter, the newly created rectangular block, to its correct location.

Rotating the Rectangular Block

1. Select **3D Rotate** in the *Modify* toolbar as shown.

2. In the command prompt area, the message *"Select objects:"* is displayed. Select the **rectangular block** by clicking on any of the displayed edges of the model.

3. Inside the graphics window, **right-mouse-click** to accept the selection and proceed with the **3D Rotate** command.

4. In the command prompt area, the message *"Specify base point:" is displayed.* Select the **top front corner** of the rectangular box as shown.

• Note that the **3D Rotate** command requires the definition of a *base point*, a *rotation axis* and the *angle of rotation*.

5. In the command prompt area, the message *"Pick a rotation axis:"* is displayed. Select the X-axis by clicking once on the **RED grip rotate handle** as shown.

6. In the command prompt area, the message *"Specify angle start point:"* is displayed. Enter **90** [**ENTER**].

Reposition the Rectangular Block

1. **Pre-select** the rectangular block by left-clicking on any edge of the block.

2. Inside the graphics window, right-mouse-click and select **Move** in the pop-up menu. In the command prompt area, the message "*Specify base point or displacement:*" is displayed.

3. Snap to and select the **top front corner** of the rectangular block as the reference point.

4. In the command prompt area, the message "*Specify second point of displacement or <use first point as displacement>:*" is displayed. Enter **@0,15,-20 [ENTER]**.

5. On your own, use the **Free Orbit** command to examine the constructed objects.

6. On your own, perform the **Subtract** Boolean operation and complete the model.

The SteeringWheels

The SteeringWheels are tracking menus that are divided into different sections known as wedges. Each wedge on a wheel represents a single navigation tool. You can pan, zoom, or manipulate the current view of a model in different ways. The **3D SteeringWheel** and **2D SteeringWheel** (mostly used in the 2D drawing mode) have some or all of the following options:

Zoom - Adjusts the magnification of the view.
Center - Centers the view based on the position of the cursor over the wheel.
Rewind - Restores the previous view.
Forward - Increases the magnification of the view.
Orbit - Allows 3D free rotation with the left-mouse-button.
Pan - Allows panning with the dragging of the left mouse-button.
Up/Down - Allows panning with the use of a scroll control.
Walk - Allows the *walking*, which is linear motion perpendicular to the screen, through the model space.
Look - Allows rotation of the current view vertically and horizontally.

3D Steering Wheel   2D Steering Wheel

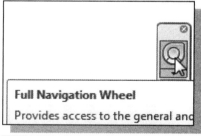

1. Activate the **SteeringWheel**, in the **View** display toolbar, by clicking on the icon as shown.

2. Move the cursor in the graphics window and notice the **3D Steering Wheel** menu follows the cursor on the screen.

3. Move the cursor on the **Orbit** option to highlight the option.

4. Click and drag with the left-mouse-button to activate the **Free Rotation** option.

5. Drag with the left-mouse-button and notice the **ViewCube** also reflects the model orientation.

6. Move the cursor to the left side of the model and click the **Center** option as shown. The display is adjusted so the selected point is the new **Zoom/Orbit** center.

7. On your own, experiment with the other available options.

Review Questions:

1. What are the three basic Boolean operations commonly used in computer geometric modeling software?

2. What is a *primitive solid*?

3. What does *CSG* stand for?

4. Which Boolean operation keeps only the volume common to the two solid objects?

5. What is the difference between a *CUT* feature and a *UNION* feature in AutoCAD?

6. Using the CSG concept, create Binary Tree sketches showing the steps you plan to use to create the two models shown on the next page:

Ex.1)

Ex.2)

Exercises: All dimensions are in inches.

1.

2.

3.

4.

5.

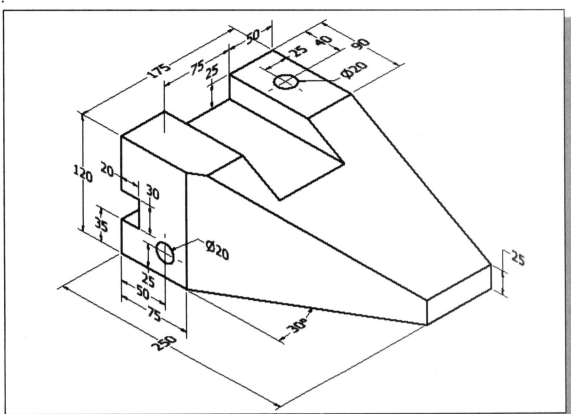

Notes:

Chapter 7
Regions, Extrude and Solid Modeling

Learning Objectives

♦ **Use 2D Extrusion Method to Create Solid Models**

♦ **Understand and Create Regions**

♦ **Edit 3D Geometry with the Rotate and Move Commands**

♦ **Examine the Mass Properties of Solids**

♦ **Understand the Concept of Boundary-Representation Modeling Approach**

Introduction

AutoCAD provides many powerful modeling and design-tools, and there are many different approaches to accomplish solid modeling tasks. The CSG approach, as illustrated in the previous chapter, allows designers to create solid models by using a set of predefined shapes to simulate the manufacturing process. Using only a limited set of predefined solids becomes less efficient as more complex geometric definitions are involved. Another solid modeling method, parallel to the development of the CSG approach, is the **Boundary Representation (B-rep)** approach. CSG defines a model in terms of combining basic solid shapes and B-rep defines a model in terms of its edges and surfaces. Two of the most important solid construction operations based on the B-rep approach are **Extrude** and **Revolve**. The Extrude and Revolve options can be used to convert two-dimensional filled polygons into 3D solid models. This concept of using two-dimensional sketches of the three-dimensional features proves to be an effective way to construct solid models. Many designs are in fact the same shape in one direction. Computer input and output devices we use today are largely two-dimensional in nature, which makes this modeling technique quite practical. AutoCAD's solid modeler is a hybrid modeler; the user interface and construction techniques are CSG-based, whereas the B-rep capabilities are invoked automatically and are transparent to the user.

It is important to point out that solid modeling provides us with very powerful design tools. With the abundant tools available in solid modeling software, the modeling techniques are limited only to the imagination of the designer. Instead of the individual 2D views, one should concentrate on the 3D features of designs. In this chapter, the *V-Block* design from chapter four is revisited to introduce the solid modeling tools available in *AutoCAD*. The procedure to creating solid models using the **Extrude** command is demonstrated.

The *V-Block-Solid* Design

> ➢ Make a rough sketch of a CSG binary tree showing the steps that can be used to construct the design. What are the advantages and limitations of using the CSG approach in creating the design? What other tools could be helpful to the modeling task at hand? Take a few minutes to consider these questions. You are encouraged to construct the design on your own prior to going through the tutorial.

Starting Up AutoCAD 2017

1. Select the **AutoCAD 2017** option on the *Program* menu or select the **AutoCAD 2017** icon on the *Desktop*.

2. In the *Startup* window, select **Start from Scratch**, as shown in the figure below.

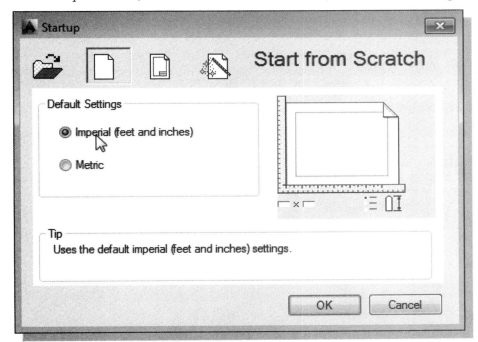

3. In the *Default Settings* section, pick **Imperial (feet and inches)** as the drawing units.

4. Pick **OK** in the *Startup* dialog box to accept the selected settings.

Layers Setup

1.   In the *Menu Bar*, select **[Tools]** → **Toolbars]** → **[AutoCAD]** → **[Layers]**.

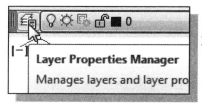

2.   Click **Layers Properties Manager** in the *Layers* toolbar.

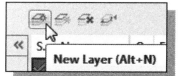

3.   Click on the **New** button to create new layers.

4.   Create **two new layers** with the following settings:

Layer	Color	Linetype	Lineweight
Construction	Grey	Continuous	Default
Object	Cyan	Continuous	0.30mm

5.   Select the layer *Construction* by clicking the layer name in the list of layers.

6.   Click on the **Current** icon to set layer *Construction* as the *Current Layer*.

7.   Click on the **Close** button to accept the settings and exit the *Layer Properties Manager* dialog box.

8.   In the *Status Bar* area, reset the options and turn *ON* the *Grid display, Polar Tracking, Object Snap, Object Snap Tracking, Dynamic Input* and *Lineweight* options.

Setting Up a 2D Sketch

1. In the *Layer Control* box, confirm layer *Construction* is set as the *Current Layer*.

2. Select the **Rectangle** icon in the *Draw* toolbar. In the command prompt area, the message *"Specify first corner point or [Chamfer/ Elevation/Fillet/Thickness/Width]:"* is displayed.

3. Place the first corner point of the rectangle near the lower left corner of the screen. Do not be overly concerned about the actual coordinates of the selected location; the CAD drawing space is as big as you can imagine.

4. We will create a 3″ × 2.25″ rectangle. Enter **@3,2.25** [**ENTER**].

❖ The Rectangle command creates rectangles as *polyline* features, which means all segments of a rectangle are created as a single object.

5. We will next make a copy of the rectangle. Pick **Copy Object** in the *Modify* toolbar.

6. Pick any edge of the rectangle we just created.

7. Inside the *graphics window*, **right-click** to accept the selection.

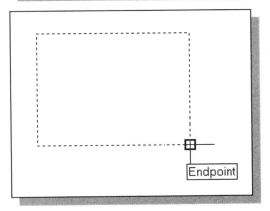

8. In the *command prompt* area, the message *"Specify base point or displacement, or [Multiple]:"* is displayed. Pick the **lower right corner** of the rectangle as the base point. A copy of the rectangle is attached to the cursor at the selected base point.

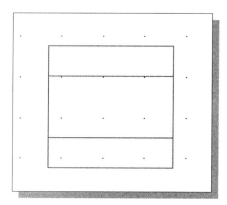

9. In the command prompt area, the message "*Specify second point of displacement, or <use first point as displacement>:*" is displayed. Enter **@0,0.75 [ENTER]**.

❖ This will position the second rectangle at the location for the 30-degree angle that is needed in the design.

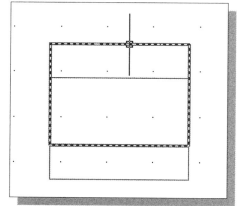

10. **Pre-select** the **copy** by picking the top horizontal line on the screen. The second rectangle, the copy we just created, is selected.

11. Pick **Rotate** in the *Modify* toolbar as shown.

12. In the command prompt area, the message "*Specify base point:*" is displayed. Pick the lower right corner of the selected rectangle as the base point.

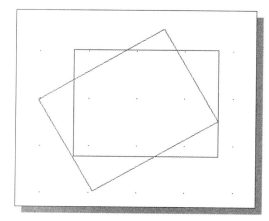

13. In the command prompt area, the message "*Specify the rotation angle or [Reference]:*" is displayed. Enter **30 [ENTER]**.

Defining the Front Edges of the Design

1. In the *Status Bar* area, **right-click** on the *POLAR* option to bring up the option menu.

2. Select **Settings** in the *option menu* as shown.

3. In the *Drafting Settings* window, confirm the *Increment angle* is set to **30** in the *Polar Angle Settings* area.

4. Switch **ON** the **Track using all polar angle settings** and **Relative to last segment** options as shown.

5. In the *Drafting Settings* window, click on the **Object Snap** tab to display and set the *Object Snap* options.

6. On your own, reset the *Object Snap modes* so that only the **Endpoint, Extension, Intersection** and **Perpendicular** are switched **ON** as shown in the figure.

7. In the *Drafting Settings* window, click **OK** to accept the settings.

*   The AutoCAD *AutoTrack*^{TM} feature includes two tracking options: *POLAR* tracking and *OBJECT SNAP* tracking. When these options are turned on, alignment markers are displayed to help us create objects at precise positions and angles.

8. On the *Object Properties* toolbar, choose the *Layer Control* box with the left-mouse-button.

9. Move the cursor over the name of layer *Object*; the tool tip "*Object*" appears. **Left-click once** and layer *Object* is set as the *Current Layer*.

10. Select the **Line** command icon in the *Draw* toolbar.

11. In the command prompt area, the message "*_line Specify first point:*" is displayed. Pick the **lower left corner** of the bottom horizontal line in the front view as the starting point of the line segments.

12. Pick the **lower right corner** of the bottom horizontal line in the front view as the second point.

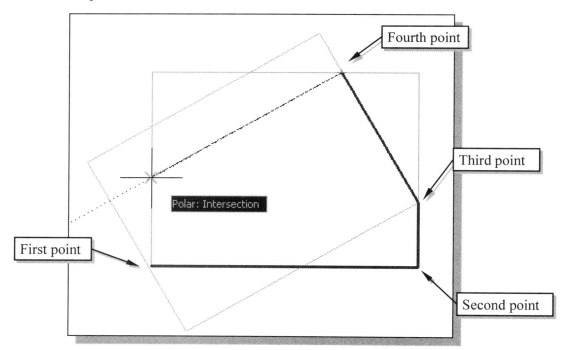

13. Select the **third** and **fourth** points as shown in the figure below.

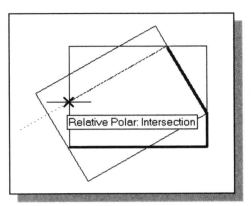

14. Move the cursor near the left vertical line and notice the *AutoTrack* feature automatically snaps the cursor to the intersection point.

15. Left-click at the intersection point as shown.

16. Inside the graphics window, right-click once to bring up the pop-up menu.

17. Pick **Close** in the pop-up menu. The Close option will create a line segment connecting the last point to the first point of the line sequence.

18. On your own, turn *OFF* the display of the *Construction Layer* by using the left-mouse-button.

19. Move the cursor into the graphics window and **left-click once** to accept the layer control settings.

Create a Region

- In AutoCAD, **regions** are 2D enclosed areas, which can be created from one or more closed shapes called **loops**. A *loop* is a curve or a sequence of connected curves that defines an area on a plane with a boundary that does not intersect itself. *Loops* can be combinations of lines, polylines, circles, arcs, ellipses, elliptical arcs, splines, 3D faces, traces, and solids. The objects that make up the loops must either be closed or form closed areas by sharing endpoints with other objects. The objects must also be coplanar, which means they must be on the same plane. We can create regions out of multiple loops and out of open curves whose endpoints are connected. Objects that intersect with themselves or with other objects cannot form regions; for example, intersecting lines, intersecting arcs or self-intersecting curves. Once a region is created, we can analyze properties such as its area and moments of inertia.

1. Select the **Region** command icon in the *Draw* toolbar.

2. In the command prompt area, the message "*Select objects:*" is displayed. Select displayed entities by creating a *selection window* enclosing **all objects**.

3. Inside the graphics window, **right-click** to accept the selection and create a region.

4. In the *View Control* list, select:

   [SE Isometric]

- Notice the orientation of the 2D region in relation to the displayed AutoCAD user coordinate system. By default, the 2D sketch-plane is aligned to the XY plane of the world coordinate system.

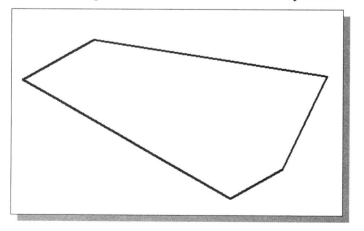

Extruding the Created Region

1. Select **Extrude** in the *3D Modeling* toolbar as shown.

2. In the command prompt area, the message *"Select objects:"* is displayed. Select the region by clicking on any of the displayed segments.

3. Inside the *graphics window*, **right-click** to accept the selection and proceed with the extrude command.

4. In the *command prompt area*, the message *"Specify height of extrusion or [path]:"* is displayed. We will extrude the region in the upward direction; enter **2.0** [**ENTER**].

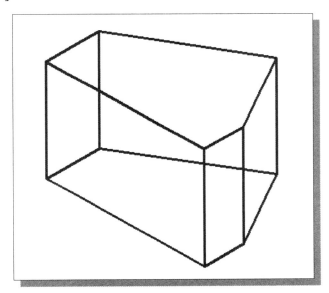

- Note that the orientation and position of solid models, in relation to the world coordinate system, can be adjusted using the Move and 3D Rotate commands.

5. Select **3D Rotate** in the *Modify* toolbar as shown.

6. In the *command prompt area*, the message *"Select objects:"* is displayed. Select the solid model by clicking on any of the displayed edges of the model.

7. Inside the graphics window, **right-click** to accept the selection and proceed with the **3D Rotate** command.

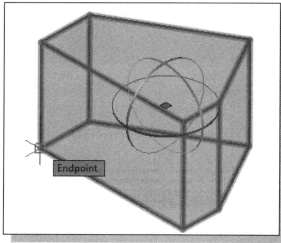

8. In the command prompt area, the message *"Specify base point:"* is displayed. Select the **lower left corner** of the model as shown.

• Note that the **3D Rotate** command requires the definition of a *base point, a rotation axis and the angle of rotation.*

9. In the command prompt area, the message *"Pick a rotation axis:"* is displayed. Select the X-axis by clicking once on the **RED grip rotate handle** as shown.

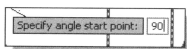

10. In the command prompt area, the message *"Specify angle start point:"* is displayed. Enter **90 [ENTER]**.

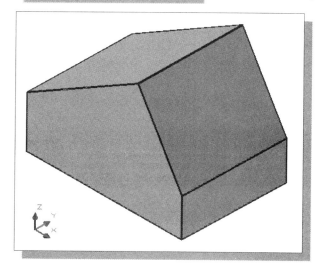

11. On your own, use the available **Visual Styles** commands to examine the created solid object.

12. On your own, reset the display to **2D Wireframe** display before proceeding to the next section.

Create a 2D Sketch at the Base of the Model

1. Select the **Line** command icon in the *Draw* toolbar. In the command prompt area, the message "*_line Specify first point:*" is displayed.

2. Inside the graphics window, hold down the [**SHIFT**] key and **right-click** once to bring up the *Object Snap* shortcut menu.

3. Select the **From** option in the pop-up window.

4. Pick the **lower right corner** of the solid model as the base point as shown in the figure.

5. We will place the first point above the selected corner. Enter **@0,0.75 [ENTER]**.

• Note the orientation of the world XY plane.

6. In the command prompt area, the message "*Specify next point or [Undo]:*" is displayed. Using the *POLAR Tracking* option (30 degrees increment), create a line that is about 1.3 inches long, as shown in the figure.

7. Move the cursor on top of the starting point of the last line to activate the *OTRACK* option and select the location that forms a 90-degrees angle as shown.

8. Inside the graphics window, right-click to activate the option menu and select **Close** with the left-mouse-button to create a line connecting to the starting point and end the **Line** command.

Create a Copy of the 2D Sketch

1. Click on the **Mirror** icon in the *Modify* toolbar.

2. In the *command prompt* area, the message *"Select objects:"* is displayed. Select the **three line segments** we just created.

3. Inside the *graphics window*, **right-click** to accept the selection and proceed with the Extrude command.

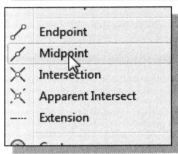

4. Inside the graphics window, hold down the [**SHIFT**] key and **right-click** once to bring up the *Object Snap* shortcut menu.

5. Select the **Midpoint** option in the pop-up window.

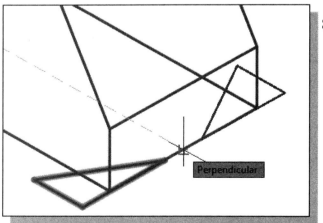

6. Click on the bottom left edge of the model. With the *Midpoint SNAP* option, the midpoint of the edge is selected.

7. Move the cursor toward the right vertical line in the active viewport, and left-click once when the **Perpendicular** tooltip is displayed as shown in the figure below.

8. In the *command prompt area*, the message *"Delete Source Objects? [Yes/No] <N>:"* is displayed. Inside the graphics window, right-click once to bring up the option menu and select **No** to keep both sets of objects.

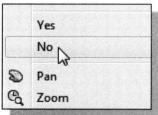

Create the Cutter Solids

- The two triangular shapes will be extruded in the Z-direction to form two solids that can be used to create the two vertical cuts.

1. Select the **Region** command icon in the *Draw* toolbar.

2. In the command prompt area, the message "*Select objects:*" is displayed. Select the **six line segments** we just created by using a selection window.

3. Inside the graphics window, **right-click** to accept the selection and create two regions.

4. Select **Extrude** in the *3D Modeling* toolbar as shown.

5. In the command prompt area, the message "*Select objects:*" is displayed. Select the **two regions** by clicking on the **two triangular regions**.

6. Inside the graphics window, right-click and select **Enter** to accept the selection and proceed with the **Extrude** command.

7. In the command prompt area, the message "*Specify height of extrusion or [path]:*" is displayed. We will extrude the regions in the upward direction; enter **2.5** [**ENTER**].

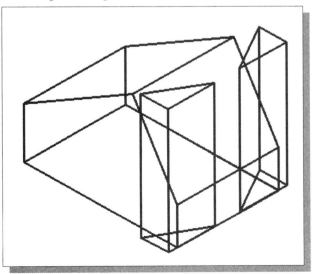

- Note that the two cutters were intentionally made larger than the dimensions shown on the design. In fact, we could create a single cutter, instead of the two we have created, provided the two triangular shapes are included and positioned at the proper locations.

Boolean Operation – *Subtract*

1. In the *Solid Editing* toolbar, click on the **Subtract** icon. In the command prompt area, the message "*_subtract Select solids and regions to subtract from ... Select Objects:*" is displayed.

2. Pick the **base block** solid by clicking on one of the edges.

3. Inside the *graphics window*, **right-click** to accept the selection and proceed with the **Subtract** command.

4. In the command prompt area, the message "*Select solids and regions to subtract... Select Objects:*" is displayed. Pick the **two triangular blocks** by clicking on the edges of the two cutters.

5. Inside the *graphics window*, **right-click** to accept the selection and proceed with the **Subtract** command.

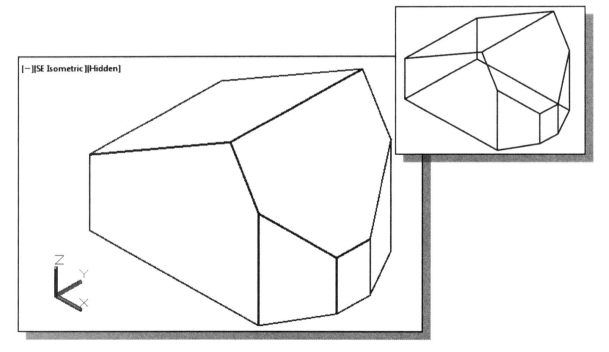

- Note that the two cut features are created fairly quickly. In comparison to the wireframe or surface models created in the previous chapters, the solid modeling approach is much more straightforward and the construction steps parallel to the manufacturing processes.

Mass Properties of the Solid Model

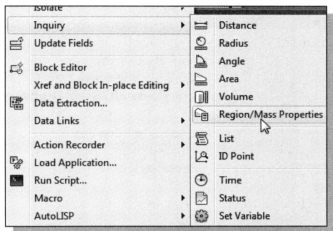

1. In the *Menu Bar*, select:

    **[Tools] → [Inquiry] →
    [Region/Mass Properties]**

2. In the *command prompt area*, the message "*Select objects:*" is displayed. Select the **solid model** by clicking on any of the displayed edges of the solid model.

3. Inside the graphics window, right-click to accept the selection and proceed with the **Region/Mass Properties** command.

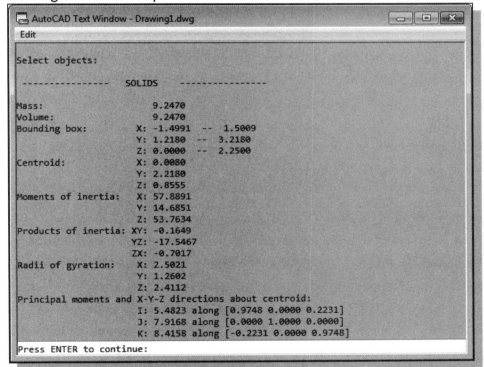

*   In the *AutoCAD Text Window*, a list of properties related to the created solid model is displayed. The *Mass* and *Volume* properties are listed as the same since a mass density of one is used for the calculation.

4. Press the [**ENTER**] key twice to close the *AutoCAD Text Window*.

Align the UCS to the Inclined Face

➢ We will create a UCS plane aligning to the inclined face of the design.

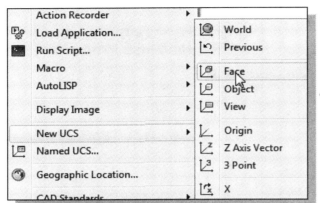

1. In the *Menu Bar*, select:

    [Tools] → [New UCS] → [Face]

    • Note that other options are also available to aid the orientation of new UCS planes.

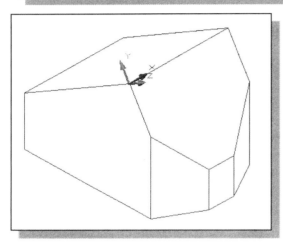

2. In the command prompt area, the message "*Select face of solid object:*" is displayed. Pick the **inclined face** by clicking on the inside of the surface and near the upper left corner.

3. Press the **[ENTER]** key to accept the new UCS positioned as shown.

4. On your own, align the UCS to the upper left corner (*UCS Origin*) as shown.

5. On your own, bring up the *UCS* toolbar.

6. In the *UCS* toolbar, select the **Z Axis Rotate** command icon as shown.

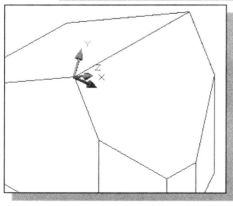

7. In the command prompt area, the message "*Specify rotation angle about Z-axis <90>:*" is displayed. Enter **-45** **[ENTER]**.

    • The negative value entered rotates the UCS clockwise about the current UCS Z-axis.

Create the *V-Cut*

1. Select the **Rectangle** icon in the *Draw* toolbar. In the command prompt area, the message "*Specify first corner point or [Chamfer/Elevation/Fillet/Thickness/Width]:*" is displayed.

2. Inside the graphics window, hold down the [**SHIFT**] key and **right-click** once to bring up the *Object Snap* shortcut menu.

3. Select the **From** option in the pop-up window.

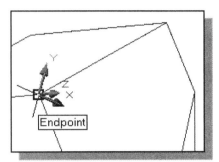

4. Pick the upper left corner of the inclined surface as the base point as shown in the figure.

5. We will place the first point above the selected corner. Enter **@0.2<45 [ENTER]**.

6. Inside the graphics window, hold down the [**SHIFT**] key and right-click once to bring up the *Object Snap* shortcut menu.

7. Select the **From** option in the pop-up window.

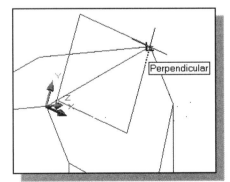

8. Pick the upper right corner of the inclined surface as the base point as shown in the figure.

9. We will place the first point above the selected corner. Enter **@0.2<-135 [ENTER]**.

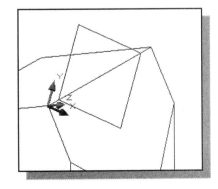

• The above procedure of creating the rectangle at the proper location is simplified by first orienting the UCS.

❖ Note that a rectangle is a valid filled polygon and therefore can be extruded into a solid object.

10. Select **Extrude** in the *Modeling* toolbar as shown.

11. In the *command prompt area*, the message *"Select objects:"* is displayed. Select the rectangle by clicking on any of the edges of the created rectangle.

12. Inside the *graphics window*, **right-click** once and select **Enter** to accept the selection and proceed with the Extrude command.

13. In the *command prompt area*, the message *"Specify height of extrusion or [path]:"* is displayed. We will extrude toward the left side of the model, to set the direction to the **negative** extrusion direction: **4.0 [ENTER]**.

- The negative number indicates the extrusion direction, which needs to be in the negative Z-direction of the current UCS.

14. In the *Modeling* toolbar, click on the **Subtract** icon. In the command prompt area, the message *"_subtract Select solids and regions to subtract from ... Select Objects:"* is displayed.

15. Pick the base solid block by clicking on one of the edges.

16. Inside the graphics window, right-click to accept the selection and proceed with the **Subtract** command.

17. In the command prompt area, the message *"Select solids and regions to subtract ... Select Objects:"* is displayed. Pick the rectangular block.

18. Inside the graphics window, right-click to accept the selection and proceed with the Subtract command.

- On your own, use the dynamic viewing commands to examine the completed solid model.

19. In the *UCS* toolbar, select the **World UCS** command icon as shown.

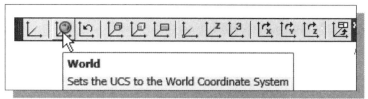

- The World UCS command aligns the UCS to the world coordinate system.

20. In the *Menu Bar*, select:
    [Tools] → [Inquiry] → [Region/Mass Properties]

21. In the *command prompt area*, the message "*Select objects:*" is displayed. Select the solid model by clicking on any of the displayed edges of the model.

22. Inside the *graphics window*, **right-click** to accept the selection. On your own, compare the displayed values to those shown on page 7-17.

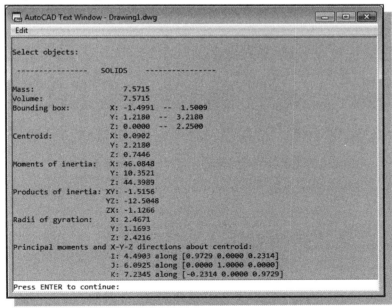

Review Questions:

1. What is an auxiliary view and why would it be important?

2. When is a line viewed as a point? When is a surface viewed as true size and shape?

3. How do we define a **Region** in AutoCAD? What are the advantages of using the Regions?

4. How is a **Solid Model** different from a **Surface Model**?

5. List some of the different mass properties that are available with 3D models in AutoCAD.

6. Identify the following commands:

    (a)

    (b)

    (c)

    (d)

Exercises: All dimensions are in inches.

1.

2.

3.

4.

5.

Notes:

Chapter 8
Multiview Drawings from 3D Models

Learning Objectives

◆ **Create Multiview Drawings from 3D Models**

◆ **Create Borders and Title Block in the Layout Mode**

◆ **Create 2D Projections from 3D Models**

◆ **Create Multiple Viewports in Paper Space**

◆ **Align and Position 2D Projected Views in Layout Mode**

Introduction

With the capabilities of solid modeling software, the importance of two-dimensional drafting is decreasing. Drafting is now considered as one of the downstream applications of using solid modeling. In many production facilities, solid models are being used to generate machine tool paths for *computer numerical control* (CNC) machine tools. Solid models can also be used in *rapid prototyping* to create 3D physical models out of plastic resins, powdered metal, etc. Ideally, the solid model database should be used directly to generate the final product. However, many organizations still require the use of two-dimensional drawings for the applications in their production facilities. In AutoCAD, model views can be used to automatically create 2D views in AutoCAD *paper space*. Using the 3D model as the starting point for a design, 3D modeling tools can easily create all the necessary two-dimensional views. In this sense, 3D modeling tools are making the process of creating two-dimensional drawings more efficient and effective.

An important rule concerning multiview drawings is to create enough views to accurately describe the design. This usually requires two or three of the regular views, such as a front view, a top view and/or a side view. Many designs have features located on inclined surfaces that are not parallel to the regular planes of projection. To truly describe the feature, the true shape of the feature must be shown using an **auxiliary view**. An *auxiliary view* has a line of sight that is perpendicular to the inclined surface, as viewed looking directly at the inclined surface. An *auxiliary view* is a supplementary view that can be constructed from any of the regular views.

In this chapter, the procedure of creating 2D drawings from 3D models is presented. We will create orthographic views, including an auxiliary view, of the *V-block* design.

The *V-Block* Design

Starting Up AutoCAD 2017

1. Select the **AutoCAD 2017** option on the *Program* menu or select the **AutoCAD 2017** icon on the *Desktop*.

2. In the AutoCAD *Startup* dialog box, select the **Open a Drawing** option with a single click of the left-mouse-button.

3. Open the *V-Block-Solid* solid model created in the previous chapter by clicking on the corresponding filename. (Use the **Browse** option to locate the solid model file if it is not displayed.)

- The *V-Block-Solid* solid model is retrieved and displayed in the graphics window.

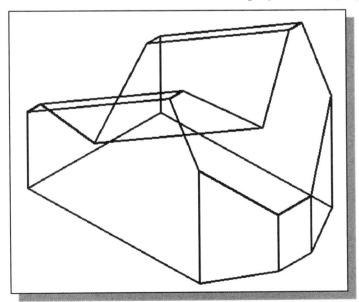

AutoCAD Paper Space

- Until now, we have been working in *model space* to create our design in <u>**full size**</u>. Once the 3D model is constructed, we can arrange our design on a two-dimensional sheet of paper so that the plotted hardcopy is exactly what we want. This two-dimensional sheet of paper is known as *paper space* in AutoCAD. We can place borders and title blocks, the objects that are less critical to our design, on *paper space*.

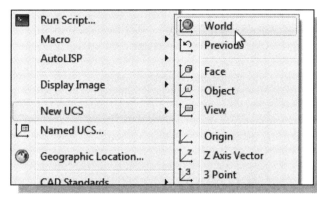

1. Set the UCS to the *World UCS* by selecting:
   [Tools] → [New UCS] → [World]

- The default 2D views generated in *paper space* are oriented based on the *World Coordinate System*. It is always a good idea to align the UCS to the WCS prior to entering the AutoCAD *paper space*.

2. Click the **Layout1** tab to switch to the two-dimensional paper space.

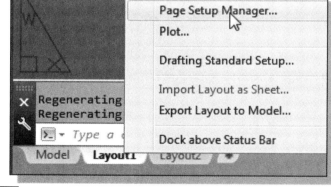

3. To adjust any *Page Setup* options, **right-click** once on the Layout1 tab and select **Page Setup Manager**.

4. Choose to **modify** the default layout in the *Page Setup Manager*.

5. In the *Page Setup* dialog box, select a plotter/printer that is available to your system. Consult with your technical support personnel if you have difficulty identifying the hardware.

6. Confirm the *Paper size* is set to **Letter** or equivalent (8.5″ by 11″) and the *Drawing orientation* is set to **Landscape**. Accept the settings and exit the *Page Setup Manager*.

❖ In the *graphics window*, a rectangular outline on a gray background indicates the paper size. The dashed lines displayed within the paper indicate the *printable area*. The 3D model appears inside a solid rectangle, which is known as a **viewport**. Note that the orientation of the model is identical to that of the model space.

Delete the Displayed Viewport

• Viewports can be considered as objects with a view into model space that we can move and resize. Floating viewports can be overlapping or separated from one another. We can also create new viewports, as well as delete them.

1. Pick **Erase** in the *Modify* toolbar.

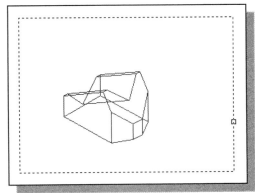

2. Pick the **viewport** by clicking on one of the edges of the viewport border.

3. Inside the graphics window, **right-click** to accept the selection and delete the viewport.

Add Borders and Title Block in the Layout

➢ **AutoCAD 2017** allows us to create plots/prints to any exact scale on the paper. We can place borders and title blocks, the objects that are less critical to our design, on *paper space*.

1. On your own, create three new layers and set *Title_Block* as the *Current Layer*.

Layer	Color	Linetype	Lineweight	Plot Style
Title_Block	Green	Continuous	1.2mm	Normal
Titleblocklettering	Green	Continuous	Default	Normal
Dimensions	Magenta	Continuous	Default	Normal
Viewport	White	Continuous	Default	Normal

2. Select the **Rectangle** icon in the *Draw* toolbar. In the command prompt area, the message *"Specify first corner point or [Chamfer/ Elevation/Fillet/Thickness/Width]:"* is displayed.

3. Pick a location that is on the inside and near the lower left corner of the dashed rectangle.

4. In the command prompt area, use the *relative coordinate entry method* and create a **10.25″ × 7.75″** rectangle.

5. Complete the title block as shown in the figure below. (Place the *text* in the *Titleblocklettering* layer.)

Setting Up Viewports inside the Title Block

- Viewports can be used in both model mode and in layout mode. In *model mode*, only *tiled viewports* (viewports cannot overlap each other) can be created. In *layout mode*, *floating viewports* (viewports can overlap each other) can be created to set up standard 2D views from 3D models.

1. In the *Object Properties* toolbar area, select the *Layer Control* box and set layer ***Viewport*** layer as the *Current Layer*.

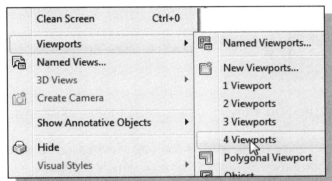

2. In the *Menu Bar*, select:
   [View] → [Viewports] → [4 Viewports].

3. In the command prompt area, the message "*Specify first corner of viewport or [Fit] <Fit>:*" is displayed. Pick a location near the lower left corner of the created border.

4. In the command prompt area, the message "*Specify opposite corner:*" is displayed. Pick a corner near the upper right corner of the border as shown.

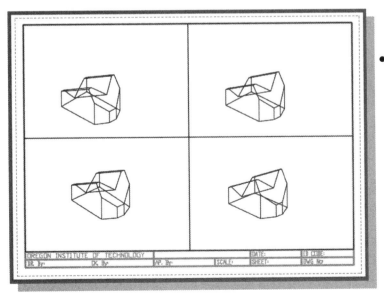

- Four viewports, with rectangular viewport borders, displaying the same Isometric view are created.

Setting Up the Standard Views

➢ AutoCAD allows us to control the display of the model inside the created viewports. This is accomplished by switching to *model mode* within each viewport. In *layout mode*, either the *paper space* is activated or one of the created viewports is activated at one time. When a viewport is activated, the *model space* of the viewport is opened, and the model mode commands become available within the viewport. The viewport with the darker border is the active viewport.

1. Move the cursor inside the **upper left viewport**.

2. **Double-click** with the left-mouse-button to activate the viewport.

- Note the darker border and the cursor display inside of the active viewport.

3. Pick the **Top** view in the *Visualize* toolbar as shown.

- The display is changed to the Top view based on the current *User Coordinate System*, which is aligned to the *WCS*.

4. Pick **Pan** in the *Quick Navigation* toolbar as shown.

5. On your own, reposition the model so that it is roughly near the center of the viewport.

- Note that the **Pan Realtime** command only adjusts the display within the active viewport. *Model space* commands are only available in the active viewport.

- On your own, experiment with other display related commands, such as Free Orbit and Zoom.

6. Move the cursor inside the lower left viewport. Left-click once inside the viewport to activate it.

7. On your own, repeat the above steps and set the four viewports to display the standard four engineering views, as shown in the figure below. (The standard four engineering views are **top**, **front**, **right**, and **isometric**.)

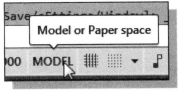

8. In the *Status Bar* area, switch back to the ***paper space*** by left-clicking once on ***MODEL***.

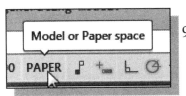

9. Click on ***PAPER*** to switch back to *model space* and note the last active viewport is activated again.

- The 3D model is displayed in all viewports; note that there is only one 3D model. The multiple viewports simply allow us to view the same model from different angles simultaneously. This approach assures the correctness and accuracy of the 2D views of the model since the views are generated from the database of the same 3D model.

Determine the Necessary 2D Views

- Multiview drawings usually require two or three of the regular views, such as a front view, a top view and/or a side view. Many designs have features located on inclined surfaces that are not parallel to the regular planes of projection. For the *V-block* design, to truly describe the V-cut feature, the true shape of the feature must be shown using an **auxiliary view**. An *auxiliary view* has a line of sight that is perpendicular to the inclined surface, as viewed looking directly at the inclined surface. An *auxiliary view* is a supplementary view that can be constructed from any of the regular views.

- Examining the current four standard views, we can conclude that the right side view provides no crucial information on the design. Instead, an *auxiliary view* is needed to truly describe the V-cut feature.

1. In the *Status Bar* area, switch back to the **paper space** by left-clicking once on **MODEL**.

2. Pick **Erase** in the *Modify* toolbar.

3. The message "*Select objects*" is displayed in the *command prompt area* and AutoCAD awaits us to select the objects to erase. Pick the **lower right viewport** by clicking on the bottom-right edge of the viewport border.

4. Inside the *graphics window*, **right-click** to accept the selection and delete the viewport.

Establish an Auxiliary View in Model Mode

➢ AutoCAD provides us with many options to establish new viewpoints. The easiest approach is to create a new UCS aligned to the inclined plane of the design and then adjust the display view to the UCS.

1. Click the **Model** tab to switch back to *model space*.

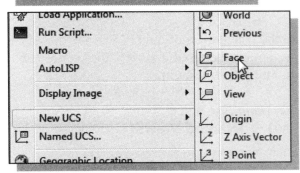

2. In the *Menu Bar*, select:
   [Tools] → [New UCS] → [Face].

3. Pick the **inclined face** by clicking on the surface near the **bottom horizontal edge** of the surface.

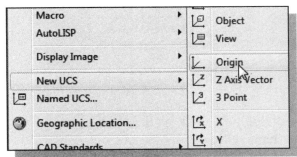

4. Press the **[ENTER]** key once to accept the new UCS.

5. In the *Menu Bar*, select:
   [Tools] → [New UCS] → [Origin].

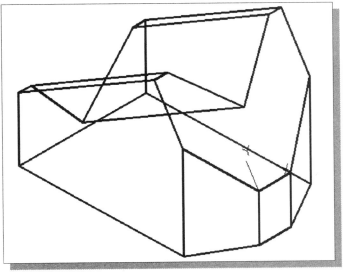

6. On your own, position the origin of the UCS to the lower left corner as shown.

7. In the *Menu Bar*, select:
    [View] → [3D Views] → [Plan View] → [Current UCS].

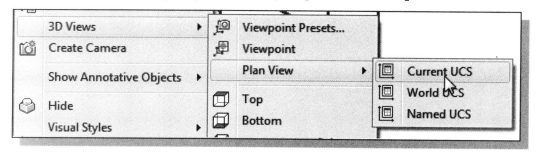

*   The graphics window is now adjusted to display the current UCS plane.

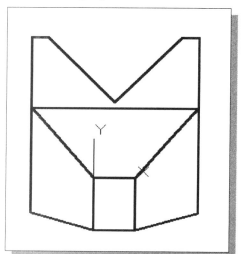

*   Note the orientation of the UCS in the display view. This is the auxiliary view that is needed in the multiview drawing.

8. In the *Menu Bar*, select:
    [View] → [Named Views].

9. In the *View* dialog box, click on the **New** button to create a new named view.

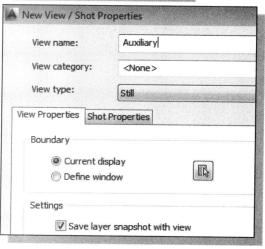

10. In the *New View* dialog box, enter **Auxiliary** as the new *View name* and confirm the ***Current display*** option and the **Save layer Snapshot with view** option are switched **ON** and the *UCS option* is set to **Unnamed** as shown.

11. Click on the **OK** button to accept the settings and create the named view.

12. In the *View* dialog box, the new named view (Auxiliary) is added to the *Named Views* list. (Note that we can also switch to this view by using the **Set Current** option.)

13. Click on the **OK** button to accept the settings.

Add a Viewport for an Auxiliary View

1. Pick the **Layout1** tab to switch back to the two-dimensional paper space.

2. In the *Status Bar* area, reset the option buttons so that only *Lineweight* is switched *ON*.

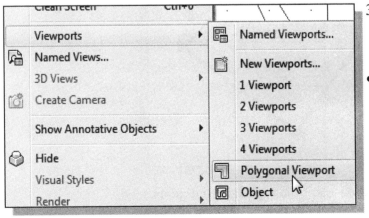

3. In the *Menu Bar*, select:
   [View] → [Viewports] → [Polygonal Viewport].

- In **AutoCAD® 2017**, viewports can be of arbitrary polygonal shapes. In the layout mode, the viewports can also overlap each other. We will create a four-sided viewport overlapping the other viewports.

4. In the command prompt area, the message "*Specify start point:*" is displayed. Create a **four-sided shape** as shown. (Hint: Use the **Close** option to assure the last segment is connected to the start point.)

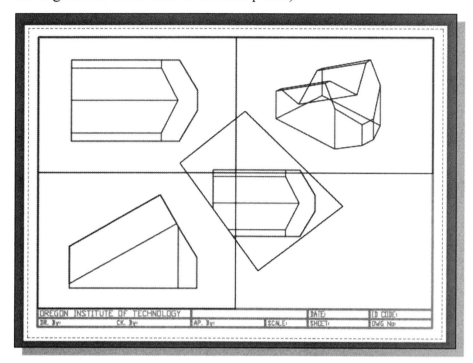

5. Pick one of the edges of the viewport border and notice that four grip points are displayed.

6. Adjust the size and shape of the viewport by dragging the grip points.

7. Press the [**Esc**] key once to deselect the highlighted objects.

8. **Double-click** inside the viewport we just created to activate the new viewport.

9. In the *Menu Bar*, select:
   [View] → [Named Views].

10. Pick the **Auxiliary** view in the *Named Views* list as shown.

11. Click on the **Set Current** to change the current display to the saved Auxiliary view.

12. Click **OK** to accept the settings.

Use the DVIEW Command

- The DVIEW command can be used to zoom, pan, and twist views. We can also use DVIEW to remove objects from in front of and behind a clipping plane and to remove hidden lines during a dynamic viewing operation.

1. At the *command prompt*, enter **dview** [**ENTER**].

2. In the command prompt area, the message "*Select objects or <use DVIEWBLOCK>:*" is displayed. Pick the **solid model** inside the active viewport.

3. Inside the active viewport, **right-click** once to accept the selection.

4. In the command prompt area, the message "*Enter option:*" is displayed. Choose the **Twist** option by entering: **TW** [**ENTER**].

5. In the command prompt area, the message "*Specify the view twist angle <0.00>:*" is displayed. Enter **30** [**ENTER**].

6. Press the [**ENTER**] key once to end the DVIEW command.

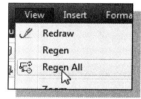

7. In the *Menu Bar*, select:
    [View] → [Regen All].

Adjust the Viewport Scale

- A uniform scale for the 2D views is necessary for view alignments and dimensioning the features.

1. Left-click in the *Status Bar* area, and switch back to the ***paper space*** mode.

2. Pre-select all **viewports** by using a selection window.

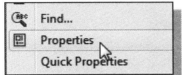

3. **Right-click** once to display the option menu.

4. Pick **Properties** in the *Standard* toolbar as shown.

5. In the *Properties* window, click on the **Quick Select** icon.

- The Quick Select option allows us to select items based on the object properties.

6. In the *Quick Select* window, choose **Layer** in the *Properties* list and set the selection operation to **Equal Viewport** as shown in the figure.

7. Click **OK** to accept the setting and proceed to select objects matching the quick select settings.

8. Choose the **4 viewports** in the selection list as shown.

9. Pick the ***Standard scale*** property in the *Misc* list as shown.

10. Select **1:1** to set the scale to one to one. This will set all displayed views to *full scale*.

11. Move the cursor inside the graphics window, and hit the [**Esc**] key once to deselect the 4 viewports.

Lock the Base View

1. Select the **lower left viewport** by clicking on one of the viewport borders.

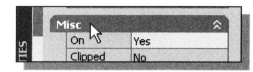

2. Find the **Misc** tab in the *Properties* palette as shown.

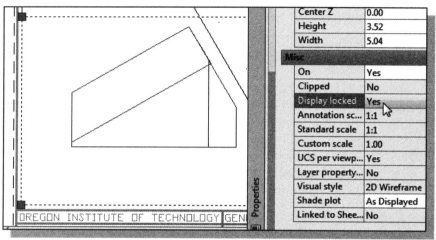

3. Pick ***Display locked*** option in the *Property* lists.

4. Set the option to **Yes** as shown.

5. Close the *Properties* window by clicking on the [**X**].

- By setting the *lock* option, the displayed view is locked at its current location. We will use this view as the base view.

Align the 2D Views

- We will create two construction lines to assist the alignments of the 2D views.

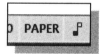

1. Confirm that the *paper space* is active. Click on the MODEL button if it is not set to the *paper space*.

2. Confirm **Viewport layer** is set as the *current layer* as shown.

3. Choose the **Construction Line** command in the *Draw toolbar* as shown.

4. On your own, create two lines aligned to the upper left corner of the front view as shown. (Hint: turn *ON* the *OSNAP* and *AUTOTRACK* options to help the constructions.)

5. **Double-click** inside the upper left viewport to activate the viewport.

6. Activate the **Pan Realtime** command by moving the cursor inside the graphics area and pressing down the mouse wheel.

7. On your own, reposition the displayed Top view so that it is aligned vertically to the Front view. Use the vertical construction line to assist the alignment.

8. Repeat the above steps and reposition the Auxiliary view so that it is aligned to the Front view as shown in the figure below.

9. Turn **OFF** layer *Viewport* and layer *Construction* and set the **Dimensions** layer as the active layer in the *Layer Control* box as shown.

•   Note that the viewport borders and the two construction lines are switched *OFF* since they are placed in the layer *Viewport*.

10. **Double-click** on the inside of the Isometric view and note the upper right viewport is activated.

11. Click **Zoom Realtime** in the *Standard* toolbar as shown.

12. On your own, resize and reposition the Isometric view so that it does not overlap with the Auxiliary view.

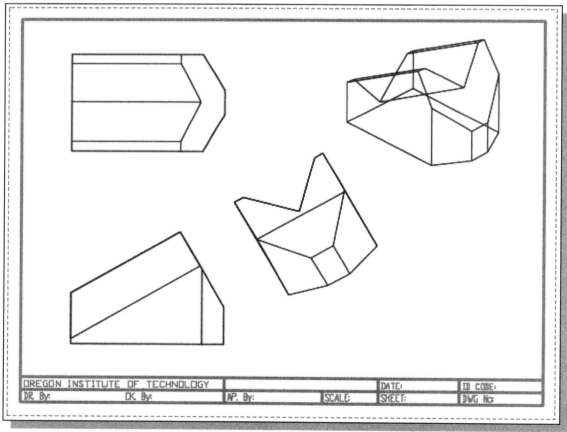

Create 2D Projected Entities – SOLPROF

- The views created so far are still 3D in nature. This prevents us from setting color or linetype for individual edges, so that hidden features can be described correctly based on engineering drafting standards. To overcome this problem, we will generate 2D entities from the established viewports. We can then use layer controls to set color and linetype options, which allows us to distinguish visible and hidden objects in individual views.

  1. **Double-click** inside the **lower left viewport** to activate the viewport.

  2. At the *command prompt*, enter **solprof** [ENTER].

  3. In the command prompt area, the message "*Select objects:*" is displayed. Pick the **solid model** inside the active viewport.

  4. Inside the active viewport, **right-click** once to accept the selection.

  5. In the command prompt area, the message "*Display hidden profile lines on separate layer? [Yes/No] <Y>:*" is displayed. Click **Yes** in the *prompt area* or enter **Y** [ENTER].

  6. In the command prompt area, the message "*Project profile lines onto a plane? [Yes/No] <Y>:*" is displayed. Click **Yes** in the *prompt area* or enter **Y** [ENTER].

  7. In the command prompt area, the message "*Delete tangential edges? [Yes/No] <Y>:*" is displayed. Click **Yes** in the *prompt area* or enter **Y** [ENTER].

- The display in the layout appears to be the same before the SOLPROF command was executed. Projected 2D entities (profile lines) are created in the view direction of the viewport.

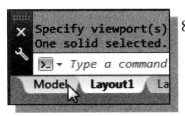

  8. Pick the **Model** tab to switch back to the 3D *model space*.

- The projected 2D entities appear in *model space*. Note that the locations of the projected entities might be at a different location on your screen than is displayed in the figure.

9. Pick the **Layout1** tab to switch back to the two-dimensional *paper space*.

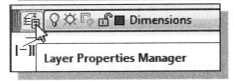

10. Click on the **Layer Properties Manager** icon in the *Layers* toolbar.

- Note that two additional layers are created by the SOLPROF command. The *PV-xx* layer is for the projected visible lines and *PH-xx* layer is for the projected hidden lines.

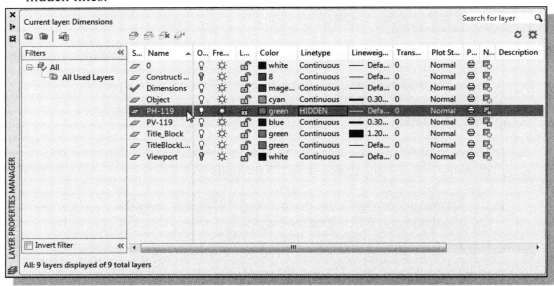

11. On your own, change the two layers to the following settings:

Layer	Color	Linetype	Lineweight	Plot Style
PH-xx	Green	HIDDEN	Default	Normal
PV-xx	Blue	Continuous	0.3mm	Normal

12. On your own, *Freeze* the layer *Object* to remove the solid object from the display.

13. Click the **Close** button to accept the settings.

- Note that only the projected entities are displayed.

14. On your own, *Thaw* the *Object* layer and repeat the above steps to generate 2D projected entities for the other three views. Also turn off the hidden layers for the Auxiliary and isometric views.

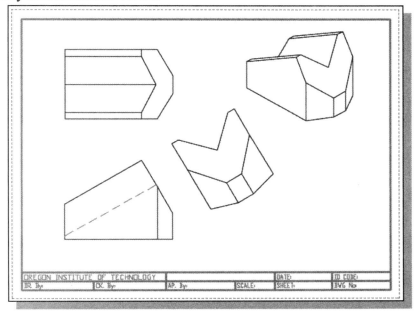

Complete the 2D Drawing

- Dimensions and notes can be placed in the *model space* or the *paper space*. From a design/modeling perspective, it is generally agreed that the dimensions should be placed in the 2D *paper space*.

1. Confirm the active mode is set to *paper space* as shown in the *Status Bar* area.

2. Confirm the *Dimensions* layer is set as the *Current Layer* in the *Layer Properties* box.

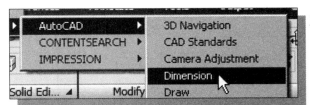

3. Select **Tool → Toolbar → AutoCAD →   Dimension** to display the *Dimension* toolbar on the screen.

4. On your own, create the necessary dimensions and complete the 2D drawing as shown.

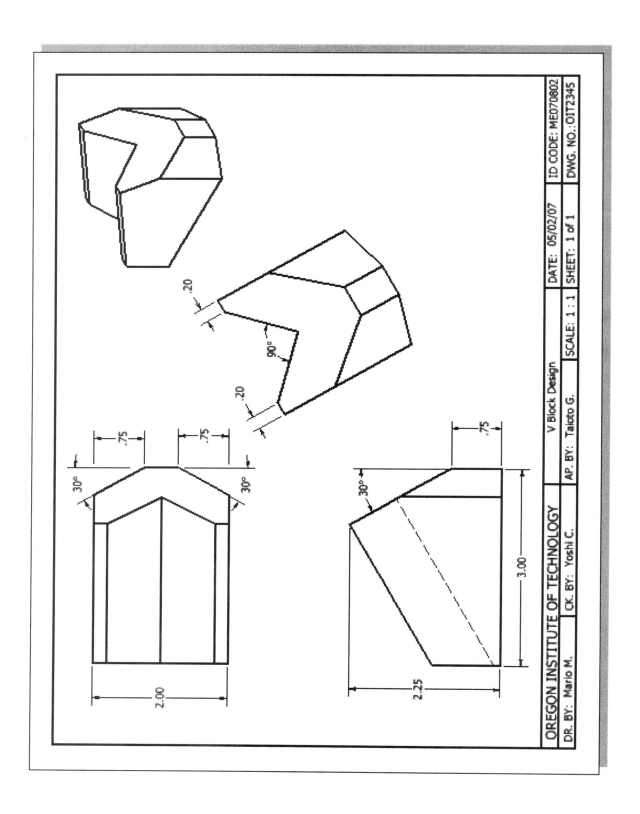

OREGON INSTITUTE OF TECHNOLOGY

V Block Design

DATE: 05/02/07

ID CODE: ME070802

DWG. NO.: OIT2345

DR. BY: Mario M.

CK. BY: Yoshi C.

AP. BY: Taioto G.

SCALE: 1 : 1

SHEET: 1 of 1

Review Questions:

1. What is an auxiliary view and why would it be important?

2. List and describe the types of 2D views used in the lesson.

3. Why and when should you use the **SOLPROF** command?

4. What is the difference between *model space* and *paper space* in AutoCAD?

5. Why and when should you use the **DVIEW** command?

6. Identify the following commands:

    (a)

    (b)

    (c)

    (d)

    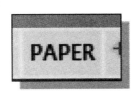

Exercises: Create the following solid models and generate multiview drawings from the 3D models. (All dimensions are in inches.)

1.

2.

3.

4.

5. Rounds: R.75

Chapter 9
Symmetrical Features in Designs

Learning Objectives

♦ **Create Revolved Features**
♦ **Use the Mirror Part Command**
♦ **Understand and Create Construction Geometry**
♦ **Create Combined Parts**
♦ **Create and Modify Feature Arrays**
♦ **Understand the Importance of Identifying Symmetrical Features in Designs**

Introduction

In solid modeling, it is important to identify and determine the features that exist in the design. *Modern solid modeling systems* enable us to build complex designs by working on smaller and simpler units. This approach simplifies the modeling process and allows us to concentrate on the characteristics of the design. Symmetry is an important characteristic that is often seen in designs. Symmetrical features can be easily accomplished by the assortments of tools that are available in feature-based modeling systems, such as AutoCAD.

The modeling technique of extruding two-dimensional sketches along a straight line to form three-dimensional features, as illustrated in the previous chapters, is an effective way to construct solid models. For designs that involve cylindrical shapes, shapes that are symmetrical about an axis, revolving two-dimensional sketches about an axis can form the needed three-dimensional features. In solid modeling, this type of feature is called a **revolved feature**.

In AutoCAD, besides using the **Revolve** command to create revolved features, several options are also available to handle symmetrical features. For example, we can create multiple identical copies of symmetrical features with the **Array** command, or create mirror images of models using the **Mirror** command. In this chapter, the construction and modeling techniques of these more advanced features are illustrated.

A Revolved Design: *Pulley*

❖ Based on your knowledge of AutoCAD, how many features would you use to create the design? Which feature would you choose as the starting point for creating the model? Identify the symmetrical features in the design and consider other possibilities in creating the design. You are encouraged to create the model on your own prior to following through the tutorial.

Modeling Strategy – A Revolved Design

Starting Up AutoCAD 2017

1. Select the **AutoCAD 2017** option on the *Program* menu or select the **AutoCAD 2017** icon on the *Desktop*.

2. In the *Startup* window, select **Start from Scratch**, as shown in the figure below.

3. In the *Default Settings* section, pick **Imperial (feet and inches)** as the drawing units.

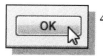
4. Pick **OK** in the *Startup* dialog box to accept the selected settings.

Layers Setup

1. In the *Menu Bar*, select **[Tools]** → **[Toolbars]** → **[AutoCAD]** → **[Layers]**.

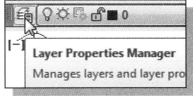

2. Click **Layers Properties Manager** in the *Layers* toolbar.

3. Click on the **New** button to create new layers.

4. Create **three new layers** with the following settings:

Layer	Color	Linetype	Lineweight
Center_lines	Red	Center	Default
Dimensions	Magenta	Continuous	Default
Object_lines	Cyan	Continuous	0.3mm

S...	Name	O...	Freeze	L...	Color	Linetype	Lineweight	Trans...	Plc
✓	0	💡	☼	🔓	white	Continuous	—— Default	0	No
	Center_lines	💡	☼	🔓	red	CENTER	—— Default	0	No
	Dimensions	💡	☼	🔓	mage...	Continuous	—— Default	0	No
	Object_lines	💡	☼	🔓	cyan	Continuous	▬ 0.30 mm	0	No

5. Select *Object_lines* layer in the list of layers.

6. Click on the **Current** button to set layer *Object_lines* as the *Current Layer*.

7. Click on the **Close** button to accept the settings and exit the *Layer Properties Manager* dialog box.

8. In the *Status Bar* area, reset the options and turn *ON* the *Polar Tracking, Object Snap, Object Snap Tracking, and Dynamic Input* options.

Set Up a 2D Sketch for the Revolved Feature

- Note that the *Pulley* design is symmetrical about a horizontal axis as well as a vertical axis, which allows us to simplify the 2D sketch as shown below. Instead of creating the 2D sketch by the **Line** command, we will use some of the more advanced editing options available with the **Region** command.

1. Select the **Rectangle** icon in the *Draw* toolbar. In the command prompt area, the message "*Specify first corner point or [Chamfer/ Elevation/Fillet/ Thickness/Width]:*" is displayed.

2. Place the first corner point of the rectangle near the center of the screen. Do not be overly concerned about the actual coordinates of the selected location; the CAD drawing space is as big as you can imagine.

3. We will create a 0.75″ × 1.625″ rectangle for the main body of the sketch. Enter **@.75,1.625 [ENTER]**.

4. Inside the graphics window, click once with the right-mouse-button to bring up the pop-up option menu.

5. Pick **Repeat Rectangle**, with the left-mouse-button, in the pop-up menu to repeat the last command.

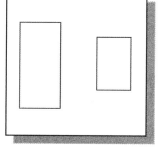

6. Place the first corner point of the rectangle toward the right side of the previous rectangle.

7. We will create a 0.625″ × 1.0″ rectangle as a cutter sketch. Enter **@.625,1 [ENTER]**.

8. Select the **Move** icon in the *Modify* toolbar.

9. In the command prompt area, the message *"Select Objects:"* is displayed. Pick the cutter rectangle, **the smaller rectangle**, to move.

10. Inside the graphics window, **right-click** to accept the selection.

11. In the command prompt area, the message *"Specify base point or displacement:"* is displayed. Pick the **upper left corner** of the smaller rectangle as shown.

12. Inside the graphics window, hold down the [**SHIFT**] key and **right-click** once to bring up the *Object Snap* shortcut menu.

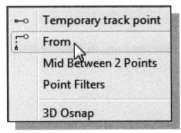

13. Select the **From** option in the pop-up window.

14. Pick the upper left corner of the larger rectangle as shown.

15. In the command prompt area, the message *"Specify base point or displacement: _from Base point: <Offset>:"* is displayed. Enter **@.125,-.25 [ENTER]**.

16. Pre-select the **smaller rectangle** to activate the grip-editing function.

17. Pick the **lower right grip point** displayed along the right vertical edge.

18. Inside the graphics window, hold down the [**SHIFT**] key and **right-click** once to bring up the *Object Snap* shortcut menu.

19. Select the **From** option in the pop-up window.

20. Pick the **lower right corner** of the larger rectangle.

21. At the command prompt: **@0,.125 [ENTER]**.

22. Press the [**Esc**] key once to deselect any selected entities.

Perform 2D Boolean Operations

- AutoCAD's 2D regions are special types of filled polygons. We can create composite 2D regions by applying *Boolean operations* to subtract, find the intersection, or combine two or more regions.

1. Select the **Region** command icon in the *Draw* toolbar.

2. In the *command prompt area*, the message "*Select objects:*" is displayed. Select the **polygon** we just edited.

3. Inside the *graphics window*, **right-click** to accept the selection and create a region.

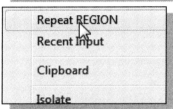

4. Inside the *graphics window*, click once with the right-mouse-button to bring up the pop-up option menu.

5. Pick **Repeat Region**, with the left-mouse-button, in the pop-up menu to repeat the last command.

6. In the command prompt area, the message "*Select objects:*" is displayed. Select the **rectangle** by clicking on one of the edges.

7. Inside the graphics window, **right-click** to accept the selection and create a region.

8. In the *Modeling* toolbar, click on the **Subtract** icon. In the command prompt area, the message "*_subtract Select solids and regions to subtract from .,. Select Objects:*" is displayed.

9. Pick the **rectangle** by clicking on one of the edges.

10. Inside the *graphics window*, right-click to accept the selection and proceed with the Subtract command.

11. In the *command prompt area*, the message "*Select solids and regions to subtract ... Select Objects:*" is displayed. Pick the four-sided **polygon** by clicking on one of the edges.

12. Inside the *graphics window*, **right-click** to accept the selection and proceed with the Subtract command. The completed 2D sketch is as shown.

- AutoCAD's region is a special type of geometric entity. It was developed based on the CSG solid modeling technique and is valuable in the sense that it provides a different method to construct complex geometric shapes. In many cases, the Boolean operations are more efficient than creating geometry by entering point-to-point coordinates.

13. Select the **Rectangle** icon in the *Draw* toolbar.

14. On your own, create two arbitrary rectangles roughly positioned as shown. We will use these two rectangles to shape the upper regions of the design.

15. On your own, convert the two rectangles into **two regions**.

16. Select the **Move** icon in the *Modify* toolbar.

17. In the *command prompt area*, the message "*Select Objects:*" is displayed. Pick **one of the rectangles** to move.

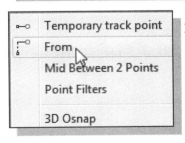

18. Inside the *graphics window*, **right-click** to accept the selection.

19. In the *command prompt area*, the message "*Specify base point or displacement:*" is displayed. Pick the **upper left corner** of the selected rectangle as shown.

20. Inside the *graphics window*, hold down the [**SHIFT**] key and **right-click** once to bring up the *Object Snap* shortcut menu.

21. Select the **From** option in the pop-up window.

22. Pick the upper left corner of the larger rectangle as shown.

23. In the *command prompt area*, the message "*Specify base point or displacement: _from Base point: <Offset>:*" is displayed. Enter **@.5,0** [ENTER].

24. On your own, perform the Boolean **Subtract** operation and create the 2D sketch as shown.

25. Select the **Rotate** icon in the *Modify* toolbar.

26. In the *command prompt area*, the message "*Select Objects:*" is displayed. Pick the **rectangle** to rotate.

27. Inside the *graphics window*, **right-click** to accept the selection.

28. In the *command prompt area*, the message "*Specify base point or displacement:*" is displayed. Pick the **inside corner** of the 2D sketch as shown.

29. Inside the *graphics window*, hold down the [SHIFT] key and **right-click** once to bring up the *Object Snap* shortcut menu.

30. Select the **From** option in the pop-up window.

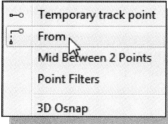

31. Pick the upper right corner of the 2D sketch as shown.

32. At the *command prompt*: **@0,-.125** [ENTER].

33. Select the **Move** icon in the *Modify* toolbar.

34. In the command prompt area, the message "*Select Objects:*" is displayed. Pick the rotated rectangle to move.

35. Inside the graphics window, right-click to accept the selection.

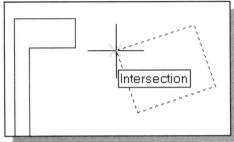

36. In the command prompt area, the message "*Specify base point or displacement:*" is displayed. Pick the upper left corner of the selected rectangle as shown.

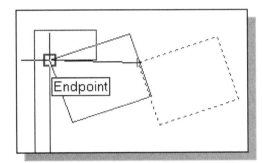

37. In the command prompt area, the message "*Specify base point or displacement:*" is displayed. Pick the inside corner of the 2D sketch as shown.

38. On your own, perform the Boolean **Subtract** operation and complete the 2D sketch as shown.

39. On your own, create a line that is ⅜ below the 2D sketch as shown. This line will be used as the axis of rotation for the revolved feature. **Trim** the line so that the **left endpoint is aligned to the left edge of the 2D sketch**.

Create the Revolved Feature

1. Select **Revolve** in the *Modeling* toolbar as shown.

2. In the command prompt area, the message "*Select objects:*" is displayed. Select the **2D region** by clicking on any of the displayed segments.

3. Inside the graphics window, **right-click** and select **Enter** to accept the selection and proceed with the Revolve command.

4. In the command prompt area, the message "*Define axis by [Object/X (axis)/Y (axis)}]:*" is displayed. Pick the **left endpoint of the centerline** as shown.

5. In the command prompt area, the message "*Specify endpoint of axis:*" is displayed. Pick the **right endpoint of the centerline**.

6. In the command prompt area, the message "*Specify angle of revolution <360>:*" is displayed. Enter **360 [ENTER]**.

*   The revolved part is created as shown.

Mirrored Image of the Part

• In AutoCAD, we can mirror a 2D sketch or a 3D part about a line or a specified surface. We can define the line by selecting existing points or by picking locations on the screen. We can physically flip the part about a reference plane or create a new mirrored part.

1. On your own, change the display to **SW Isometric View** or use the **Free Orbit** command to display the flat face of the solid model as shown.

2. In the *Modify* toolbar, select **3D Mirror**.

3. In the *command prompt area*, the message "*Select objects:*" is displayed. Select any edge of the **3D model**.

4. Inside the *graphics window*, **right-click** to accept the selection.

5. In the *command prompt area*, the message "*Specify first point of mirror plane (3 points) or [Object/Last/Zaxis/View/XY/YZ/ZX/3points] <3points>:*" is displayed. Choose the YZ plane by selecting **YZ** in the *prompt area* or enter **YZ [ENTER]**.

6. In the *command prompt area*, the message "*Select point on YZ plane <0,0,0>:*" is displayed. Pick the **left endpoint of the centerline**.

7. In the *command prompt area*, the message "*Delete source objects? [Yes/No] <N>:*" is displayed. Inside the graphics window, right-click to bring up the option menu and select **No** to create a new part.

Combine Two Parts into One

- We have created a separate part with the **Mirror 3D** command. We will combine the two parts into a single part using the CSG *Boolean operations*.

1. Select **2D Wireframe** by left-clicking once on the icon in the *Visual Style* controls list.

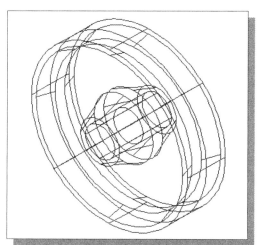

- Note the edges separating the two parts displayed on the screen.

2. Pick **Union** in the *Modeling* toolbar as shown.

3. In the *command prompt area*, the message "*Select Objects:*" is displayed. Pick the two parts.

4. Inside the *graphics window*, right-click to accept the selection and proceed with the **Union** command to combine the two parts into a single part.

- Reset the display to **2D Wireframe** mode before proceeding to the next section.

Use the 3D Array command

- In AutoCAD, existing 2D and/or 3D features can be easily duplicated. The **Array** command allows us to create both rectangular and polar arrays of features.

1. In the *View* toolbar, select the **Top** view option to reset the display.

2. Select the **Rectangle** icon in the *Draw* toolbar.

3. On your own, create a rectangle that is **1.0″ × .25″** toward the right side of the solid model.

4. On your own, convert the rectangle into a *region*.

- The rectangle will be used to create a cylindrical solid model. The cylinder will be used to generate a polar array using the **Array** command.

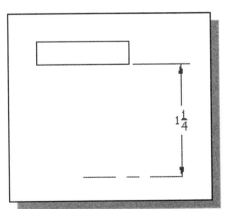

5. On your own, create a centerline that is **1¼″** below the rectangle with the **left endpoint aligned to the center of the rectangle** as shown.

- The centerline will be used as the axis of rotation to create the *polar array*.

6. Select **Revolve** in the *Modeling* toolbar as shown.

7. In the *command prompt area*, the message "*Select objects:*" is displayed. Select the **rectangular region** by clicking on any of the displayed segments.

8. Inside the graphics window, **right-click** and pick **Enter** to accept the selection and proceed with the Revolve command.

9. In the command prompt area, the message "*Define axis by [Object/X (axis)/Y (axis)}]:*" is displayed. Pick the **lower left corner** of the region as shown.

10. In the command prompt area, the message "*Specify endpoint of axis:*" is displayed. Pick the **lower right corner** of the region.

11. In the command prompt area, the message "*Specify angle of revolution <360>:*" is displayed. Enter **360.0 [ENTER]**.

12. In the *View Controls* list, click on the **SE Isometric** view icon.

13. In the standard pull-down menu, select **[Modify]** → **[3D Operations]** → **[3D Array]**.

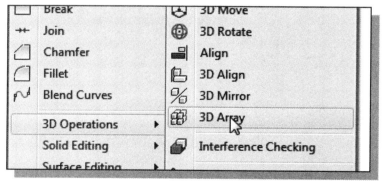

14. In the command prompt area, the message "*Select objects:*" is displayed. Select the **small cylinder** by clicking on any edge of the cylinder.

15. Inside the graphics window, **right-click** to accept the selection.

16. In the command prompt area, the message *"Enter the type of array [Rectangular/ Polar] <R>:"* is displayed.
Choose the *Polar* option by selecting **Polar** in the *prompt area* or enter **P** [**ENTER**].

17. In the command prompt area, the message *"Enter the number of items in the array:"* is displayed. We will create 6 items by entering **6** [**ENTER**].

18. In the command prompt area, the message *"Specify the angle to fill (+=ccw, - =cw) <360>:"* is displayed. Enter **360** [**ENTER**].

19. In the command prompt area, the message *"Rotate arrayed objects?[Yes/No] <Y>:"* is displayed. Click **No** in the prompt area or enter **N** [**ENTER**].

20. In the command prompt area, the message *"Specify center point of array:"* is displayed. Pick the **left endpoint of the centerline** as shown.

21. In the command prompt area, the message *"Specify second point on axis of rotation:"* is displayed. Pick the right endpoint of the centerline as shown.

Position and Perform the Cut

1. Select the **Move** icon in the *Modify* toolbar.

2. In the command prompt area, the message "*Select Objects:*" is displayed. Pick the **six cylinders** we just created.

3. Inside the graphics window, **right-click** to accept the selection.

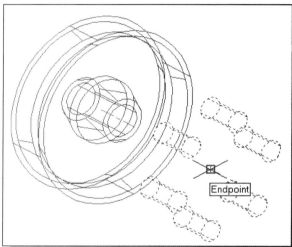

4. In the command prompt area, the message "*Specify base point or displacement:*" is displayed. Pick the **left endpoint of the polar array centerline** as shown.

5. In the command prompt area, the message "*Specify base point or displacement:*" is displayed. Pick the **left endpoint of the centerline** of the *Pulley* as shown.

6. In the *Modeling* toolbar, click on the **Subtract** icon.

7. In the *command prompt area*, the message "*_subtract Select solids and regions to subtract from ... Select Objects:*" is displayed. Pick the **Pulley** model by clicking on one of the edges.

8. Inside the graphics window, **right-click** to accept the selection and proceed with the Subtract command.

9. In the command prompt area, the message "*Select solids and regions to subtract ... Select Objects:*" is displayed.

10. Pick the **six cylinder** blocks by clicking on their circular edges.

11. Inside the graphics window, right-click to accept the selection and proceed with the Subtract command.

• On your own, create the 2D drawing from the 3D model as shown.

Review Questions:

1. List the different symmetrical features created in the *Pulley* design.

2. What are the advantages of using *regions*?

3. Describe the steps required in using the **Mirror Part** command.

4. Why is it important to identify symmetrical features in designs?

5. When and why should we use the **Array** option?

6. What is the difference between *Rectangular Array* and *Polar Array*?

7. When and why should you use the **Revolve** command in AutoCAD?

8. Identify and describe the following commands:

(a)

(b)

(c)

(d)

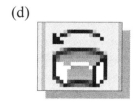

Exercises:

1. Dimensions are in inches.

2. Dimensions are in inches. Plate thickness : 0.25 inch

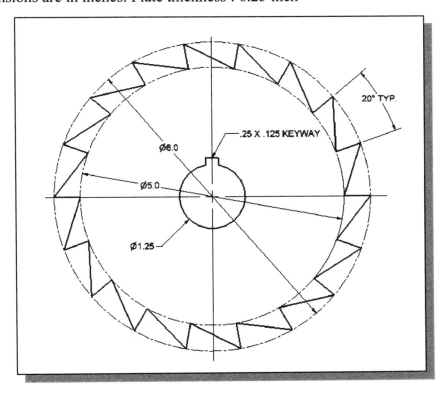

3. Dimensions are in inches.

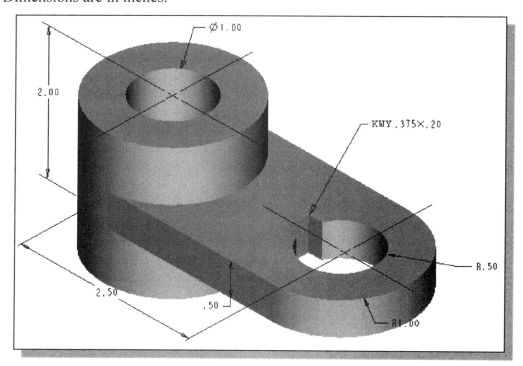

4. Dimensions are in inches.

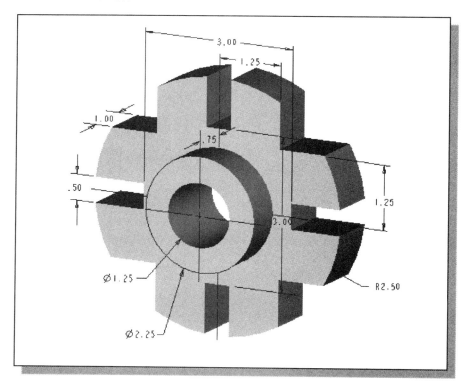

5. Dimensions are in inches.

Notes:

Chapter 10
Advanced Modeling Tools & Techniques

Learning Objectives

♦ **Use More Advanced Solid Modeling Construction Tools**
♦ **Create Draft Angle Features**
♦ **Use the 3D Rounds & Fillets Command**
♦ **Create Rectangular Patterns**
♦ **Use the Shell Command**
♦ **Use the Copy Faces Command**
♦ **Use the DUCS Option**

Introduction

AutoCAD provides an assortment of three-dimensional construction tools to make the creation of solid models easier and more efficient. In this chapter, we will examine the procedures to create the *Draft Angle* feature, the *Shell* feature and also for creating three-dimensional *Rounds* and *Fillets* along edges of a solid model. These features are common characteristics of molded parts. The three-dimensional **Fillets** and the **Shell** commands will usually create complex three-dimensional spatial curves and surfaces. These commands are more sensitive to the associated geometric entities. For this reason, the *3D Fillets* and the *Shell* features are typically created last after all associated solid features are created. In this chapter, we will also examine the new tools available in AutoCAD 2017 for referencing to existing surfaces and the enhancement of the **Grip editing** tools.

A Thin-Walled Design: *Oil Sink*

❖ Based on your knowledge of AutoCAD so far, how many features would you use to create the design? Which feature would you choose as the starting point in creating the model? What are the more difficult features involved in the design? What is your choice in arranging the order of the features? Take a few minutes to consider these questions and do preliminary planning by sketching on a piece of paper. You are also encouraged to create the design on your own prior to following through the tutorial.

Modeling Strategy

Starting Up AutoCAD 2017

1. Select the **AutoCAD 2017** option on the *Program* menu or select the **AutoCAD 2017** icon on the *Desktop*.

2. In the *Startup* window, select **Start from Scratch**, as shown in the figure below.

3. In the *Default Settings* section, pick **Imperial (feet and inches)** as the drawing units.

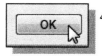

4. Pick **OK** in the *Startup* dialog box to accept the selected settings.

Layers Setup

1. In the *Menu Bar,* select **[Tools]** → **[Toolbars]** → **[AutoCAD]** → **[Layers]**.

2. Click **Layers Properties Manager** in the *Layers* toolbar.

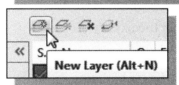

3. Click on the **New** button to create new layers.

4. Create **three new layers** with the following settings:

Layer	Color	Linetype	Lineweight
Center_lines	Red	Center	Default
Dimensions	Magenta	Continuous	Default
Object_lines	Cyan	Continuous	0.3mm

5. Select *Object_lines* layer in the list of layers.

6. Click on the **Current** button to set layer *Object_lines* as the *Current Layer*.

7. Click on the **Close** button to accept the settings and exit the *Layer Properties Manager* dialog box.

8. In the *Status Bar* area, reset the options and turn *ON* the *Polar Tracking, Object Snap, Object Snap Tracking, and Dynamic Input* options.

The First Extruded Feature

1. Select the **Rectangle** icon in the *Draw* toolbar. In the command prompt area, the message "*Specify first corner point or [Chamfer/ Elevation/Fillet/Thickness/Width]:*" is displayed.

2. Place the first corner point of the rectangle near the lower left corner of the screen.

3. We will create a *16″* **x** *12″* rectangle for the main body of the sketch. Enter **@16,12 [ENTER]**.

4. Select the **Fillet** command icon in the *Modify* toolbar. In the command prompt area, the message "*Select first object or [Polyline/Radius/Trim]:*" is displayed.

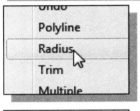

5. Inside the graphics window, right-click to activate the option menu and select the **Radius** option with the left-mouse-button to specify the radius of the fillet.

6. In the command prompt area, the message "*Specify fillet radius:*" is displayed. *Specify fillet radius:* **4 [ENTER]**.

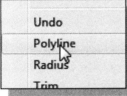

7. Inside the graphics window, right-click to activate the option menu and select the **Polyline** option.

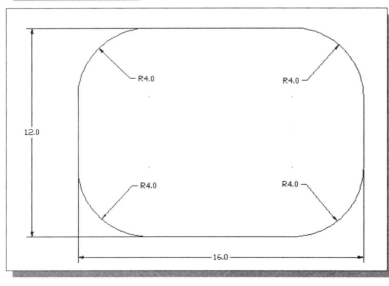

8. Pick the rectangle to create the **four rounded corners** as shown.

9. Select the **Region** command icon in the *Draw* toolbar.

10. In the command prompt area, the message "*Select objects:*" is displayed. Select the **polyline** by clicking on any segments of the 2D sketch.

11. Select **Extrude** in the *Modeling* toolbar as shown.

12. In the *command prompt area*, the message "*Select objects:*" is displayed. Select the region by clicking on any of the displayed segments.

13. Inside the *graphics window*, **right-click** and select **Enter** to accept the selection and proceed with the **Extrude** command.

14. In the command prompt area, the message "*Specify height of extrusion or [Direction/Path/Taper Angle]:*" is displayed. Enter **0.625 [ENTER]**.

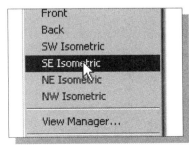

15. Set the view display to **SE Isometric** as shown.

Create an Offset Geometry from an Extracted Surface

- In AutoCAD, several options are available to create geometry from existing solid features. We will use the Copy Faces command to assist constructing geometry from the existing surfaces.

    1. In the *Menu Bar* area, select **[Tools]** → **[Toolbar]** → **[AutoCAD]** → **[Solids Editing]** as shown.

2. Click on the **Copy Faces** icon to activate the command.

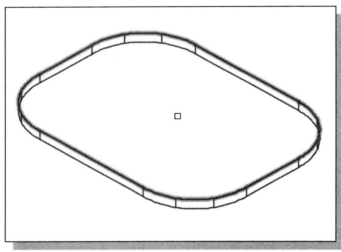

3. In the *command prompt area*, the message "*Select faces or [Undo/ Remove/ All]:*" is displayed. Pick the **upper surface** by clicking on the inside of the surface as shown.

4. Inside the graphics window, **right-click** to bring up the option menu and select **Enter** to accept the selection.

5. In the *command prompt area*, the message "*Specify a base point or displacement:*" is displayed. Select any point as a reference and enter **@20,0** to place the copy about **20** inches to the **right side** of the current model.

6. Inside the *graphics window*, **right-click** to accept the entered values.

7. In the *option menu* select **Exit**.

8. Select **Exit** again to end the Copy Faces command.

9. Select the **Explode** command icon in the *Modify* toolbar. In the command prompt area, the message "*Select objects:*" is displayed.

10. Pick the **surface** we just created.

11. Inside the graphics window, **right-click** to end the Explode command.

12. Select the **Offset** command icon in the *Modify* toolbar. In the command prompt area, the message "*Specify offset distance or [Through]:*" is displayed.
Specify offset distance or [Through]: **2** [**ENTER**].

13. On your own, create a set of entities on the **inside** of the exploded surface as shown.

14. Select the **Region** command icon in the *Draw* toolbar.

15. In the *command prompt area*, the message "*Select objects:*" is displayed. Select the **entities** we just created with the **Offset** command (the objects that form the inside loop).

16. Inside the *graphics window*, **right-click** to accept the selection and create a region.

17. Select the **Erase** command icon in the *Modify* toolbar.

18. In the *command prompt area*, the message "*Select objects:*" is displayed. Select the **outer loop entities** that were created with the *Copy Faces* command.

19. Inside the *graphics window*, **right-click** to accept the selection and end the Erase command.

Extrude with Draft Angle

1. Select **Extrude** in the *Modeling* toolbar as shown.

2. In the *command prompt area*, the message "*Select objects:*" is displayed. Select the **2D region** by clicking on any of the displayed segments.

3. Inside the *graphics window*, **right-click** and choose **Enter** to accept the selection and proceed with the **Extrude** command.

4. Inside the *graphics window*, right-click to bring up the option menu and select **Taper Angle**.

5. In the *command prompt area*, the message "*Specify angle of taper for extrusion <0>:*" is displayed. Enter **10** [**ENTER**].

6. In the *command prompt area*, the message "*Specify height of extrusion or [Direction/Path/Taper Angle]:*" is displayed. Enter **4** [**ENTER**].

- Note that the second part is created by extruding an extracted surface from the first solid model. The ability to extract and re-use existing surface-geometry is an important aspect of solid modeling. Also note that AutoCAD allows us to create multiple parts in a single drawing file, which allows us to create assembly models under the same design environment.

Align the Parts

1. Select the **Move** icon in the *Draw* toolbar.

2. In the command prompt area, the message *"Select Objects:"* is displayed. Pick the **second part** we just created.

3. Inside the graphics window, right-click to accept the selection.

4. Inside the graphics window, hold down the [**SHIFT**] key and **right-click** once to bring up the *Object Snap* shortcut menu.

5. Select the **Center** option in the pop-up window.

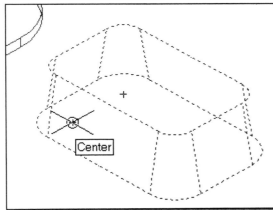

6. Pick the **center** of the bottom left arc as shown in the figure.

7. Inside the graphics window, hold down the [**SHIFT**] key and **right-click** once to bring up the *Object Snap* shortcut menu.

8. Select the **Center** option in the pop-up window.

9. Pick the corresponding center point on the **top surface** of the solid model as shown.

Create another Extracted Surface

1. Click on the **Copy Faces** icon to activate the command.

2. In the *command prompt area*, the message *"Select faces or [Undo/ Remove/ All]:"* is displayed. Pick the **top surface** of the tapered part by clicking on the inside of the surface as shown.

3. Inside the *graphics window*, **right-click** to bring up the option menu and select **Enter** to accept the selection.

4. In the *command prompt area*, the message *"Specify a base point or displacement:"* is displayed. Select any corner as a reference and enter **@20,0** to place the copy **20** inches to the right side of the current model.

5. Inside the *graphics window*, **right-click** to accept the entered values.

6. Select **eXit** in the option menu.

7. Select **eXit** in the option menu again to end the Copy Faces command.

8. Select the **Explode** command icon in the *Modify* toolbar. In the *command prompt area*, the message *"Select objects:"* is displayed.

9. Pick the **surface** we just created.

10. Inside the *graphics window*, right-click to end the Explode command.

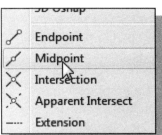

11. Select the **Line** command icon in the *Draw* toolbar.

12. Inside the graphics window, hold down the [**SHIFT**] key and **right-click** once to bring up the *Object Snap* shortcut menu.

13. Select the **Midpoint** option in the pop-up window.

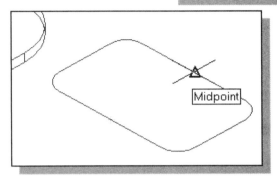

14. In the command prompt area, the message "*_line Specify first point:*" is displayed. Pick the **line segment** on the extracted surface as shown.

15. On your own, repeat the **Midpoint** *SNAP* option and create a line as shown.

16. Inside the *graphics window*, right-click once and select **Enter** to end the Line command.

17. Select the **Trim** command icon in the *Modify* toolbar.

18. In the *command prompt area*, the message "*Select boundary edges... Select objects:*" is displayed. Pick the **line** across the center of the 2D sketch.

19. Inside the *graphics window*, **right-click** to proceed with the Trim command.

20. The message "*Select object to trim or shift-select object to extend or [Project/ Edge/ Undo]:*" is displayed in the *command prompt area*. Trim the two lines of the exploded geometry as shown.

21. Select the **Region** command icon in the *Draw* toolbar.

22. In the command prompt area, the message *"Select objects:"* is displayed. Select the entities we just modified.

23. Inside the graphics window, **right-click** to accept the selection and create a region.

24. Select **Extrude** in the *3D Modeling* toolbar as shown.

25. In the command prompt area, the message *"Select objects:"* is displayed. Select the **2D region** by clicking on any of the displayed segments.

26. Inside the graphics window, right-click and select **Enter** to accept the selection and proceed with the Extrude command.

27. Inside the graphics window, right-click to bring up the option menu and select **Taper Angle**.

28. In the command prompt area, the message *"Specify angle of taper for extrusion <0>:"* is displayed. Enter **10 [ENTER]**.

29. In the command prompt area, the message *"Specify height of extrusion or [path]:"* is displayed. Enter **2 [ENTER]**.

30. Select the **Move** icon in the *Modify* toolbar.

31. On your own, reposition the part on **top** of the other parts as shown.

❖ At this point, the three separate parts are positioned and aligned on top of each other. Note that the last part was created without applying, or knowing, the exact dimensions of the extracted geometry.

Combining Parts – Boolean UNION

1. Select **Free Orbit** in the *Navigation* toolbar:
   [Orbit] → [Free Orbit].

2. On your own, rotate the created models in 3D space and confirm the three parts are positioned on top of each other. Readjust the positions of the parts if necessary.

3. In the *Solid Editing* toolbar, click on the **Union** icon. In the command prompt area, the message *"Select Objects:"* is displayed.

4. Pick all the solid models by clicking on their edges.

5. Inside the graphics window, **right-click** to accept the selection and proceed with the Union command.

Create 3D Rounds and Fillets

- In **AutoCAD 2017**, the same **Fillet** command can be applied to both 2D and 3D entities.

1. Select the **Fillet** command icon in the *Modify* toolbar.

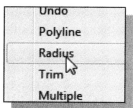

2. Inside the *graphics window*, right-click to activate the option menu and select the **Radius** option with the left-mouse-button to specify the radius of the fillet.

3. In the *command prompt area*, the message "*Specify fillet radius:*" is displayed. *Specify fillet radius:* **.75** [**ENTER**].

4. Pick the **top back edge** as shown.

5. In the *command prompt area*, the message "*Enter fillet radius <0.75>:*" is displayed. **Right-click** and choose **Enter** to accept the displayed value.

6. In the *command prompt area*, the message "*Select an edge or [Chain/Radius]:*" is displayed. **Right-click** and select **Enter** to activate the option menu and select the **Chain** option.

7. In the *command prompt area*, the message "*Select an edge or [Chain/Radius]:*" is displayed. Select one of the **adjacent curves** on the top surface.

8. On your own, select the **adjacent edges** on the top surfaces as shown in the figure.

9. Press the [**ENTER**] key or use the right-mouse-button and select **Enter** to accept the selection.

- The Fillet command can be used to create complex 3D curves and surfaces as shown in this example.

- On your own, create a *chained fillet* of **0.625 radius** at the bottom edges as shown.

Create a Shell Feature

- The **Shell** command can be used to create new faces by offsetting existing ones inside or outside of their original positions.

1. Select **Free Orbit** in the *Navigation* toolbar to the right side of the graphics area:
   [Navigation] → [Free Orbit]

2. On your own, rotate the created models in 3D space so that we are viewing the **bottom flat face** of the model as shown in the figure below.

3. Choose **Shell** in the *Solid Editing* toolbar.

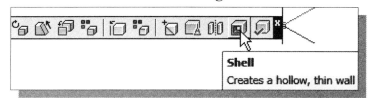

4. The message "*Select a 3D solid:*" is displayed in the command prompt area. Pick any surface of the **3D solid**. Note the entire solid is selected.

5. In the command prompt area, the message "*Remove faces or [Undo /Add /All]:*" is displayed. Select the **top flat side** (as oriented in the figure below) of the *Oil Sink* model. (AutoCAD will remove this surface before creating the shell feature.)

6. Note the message in the *command prompt area* indicating the removal of a surface. Inside the graphics window, **right-click** and select **Enter** to accept the selection and proceed with the **Shell** command.

7. In the command prompt area, the message "*Enter the shell offset distance:*" is displayed. Set the thickness to **0.25**.

8. Press the [**ENTER**] key or the **middle-mouse-button** to bring up the option menu and select **Exit** to continue.

9. Repeat the above step and **Exit** the Shell command.

Create a Rectangular Array Cut Feature

1. In the *View* control list, select the **Top** view option to reset the display to the XY plane of the coordinate system.

2. Select the **Circle** icon in the *Draw* toolbar.

3. On your own, create a circle (radius **0.375**) that is toward the right side of the solid model. Note that, in AutoCAD, *circles* are created as valid *regions*.

4. On your own, extrude the region into a **1″** high cylinder. (*Taper angle* set to **0**.)

5. Select **Rectangle Array** in the *Modify* toolbar as shown.

6. Select the **cylinder** we just created.

7. Inside the *graphics window*, **right-click** to accept the selection and proceed to use the Array command.

8. In *Columns control panel*, enter **3** as the number of items in the horizontal direction.

9. Enter **4** as the spacing between items in the horizontal direction as shown.

10. In *Columns control panel*, enter **2** as the number of items in the vertical direction.

11. Enter **10** as the distance between the rows.

12. Set the number of levels to **1** as shown.

13. Turn **Off** the **Associative** option as shown.

14. Click on **Close Array** to accept the settings and create the array.

15. Select the **Move** icon in the *Draw* toolbar, and select all six cylinders to move.

16. On your own, reposition the six cylinders as shown in the figure below. Make sure the cylinders pass through the *Oil Pan* model before proceeding to the next step.

17. In the *Solid Editing* toolbar, click on the **Subtract** icon.

18. In the *command prompt area*, the message "*_subtract Select solids and regions to subtract from ... Select Objects:*" is displayed. Pick the ***Oil Pan*** **model** by clicking on one of the edges.

19. Inside the *graphics window*, **right-click** to accept the selection and proceed with the Subtract command.

20. Pick all **six cylinder blocks** by clicking on the circular edges.

21. Inside the *graphics window*, **right-click** to accept the selection and proceed with the Subtract command.

Create another Rectangular Array Cut Feature

1. On your own, repeat the above steps and create another rectangular array as shown (circular hole: radius **0.375**, *Rectangular array*, **2** *Rows* with **4″** *Row spacing* and **2** *Columns* with **14″** *Column spacing*).

2. On your own, reposition the rectangular array so that the lower left cylinder is located at 4.0 inches away from the bottom edge of the base feature and 1.0 inch away from the left edge of the *Oil Pan* model.

3. In the *Solid Editing* toolbar, click on the **Subtract** icon.

4. In the command prompt area, the message "*_subtract Select solids and regions to subtract from ... Select Objects:*" is displayed. Pick the **Oil Pan** model by clicking on one of the edges.

5. Complete the model with the **Subtract** command.

6. Inside the graphics window, **right-click** to accept the selection and proceed with the Subtract command.

7. In the command prompt area, the message "*Select solids and regions to subtract ... Select Objects:*" is displayed.

8. Pick all **six cylinder blocks** by clicking on the circular edges.

9. Inside the graphics window, right-click to accept the selection and proceed with the Subtract command.

Making a Design Change

❖ Engineering designs usually go through many revisions and changes before they go into production. In AutoCAD 2017, an assortment of 3D tools has been implemented to handle design changes more quickly. In this section, two different approaches to perform a simple design change are illustrated: (1) modifying with the *Grip Editing* tools, and (2) creating with *Dynamic UCS*.

Grip Editing Approach: One of the main 3D editing enhancements in AutoCAD 2017 is the Grip Editing Tools. We can now use grips to manipulate original solid primitive forms that were used to make up *composite solids*. **Composite solids** are solids created from two or more individual solids through any of the *Boolean* commands: **UNION**, **SUBTRACT**, and **INTERSECT**. To select an individual form of a composite solid, press and hold the [**CTRL**] key while selecting. We will reposition the location of one of the holes using this approach.

1. Select one of the hole features by pressing down the [**CTRL**] key and clicking on one of the hole cylindrical surfaces as shown.

2. **Click** on the *center grip point* that is located at the center of the hole feature. This will activate the **Stretch** option of *Grip Editing*.

3. In the *command prompt area*, the message "*Specify stretch point or [Base point/Undo/eXit]:*" is displayed. Enter @**1.5,0** [**ENTER**].

4. On your own, use the **[Tools]** → **[Inquiry]** → **[Distance]** command to confirm the design change has been performed correctly.

Dynamic UCS Approach: In AutoCAD 2017, a new UCS tool (the **Dynamic UCS** option) was introduced, which allows quick alignment of UCS to existing surfaces. The dynamic UCS can be used to create objects on a planar face of a 3D solid without manually changing the UCS orientation. During a command, the dynamic UCS temporarily aligns the XY plane of the UCS to a planar face of a 3D solid when you move the cursor over the face. When the dynamic UCS is active, specified points, and drawing tools, such as polar tracking and the grid, are all measured relative to the temporary UCS established by the dynamic UCS. In this section, we will add an additional cylindrical solid feature on the inside wall using this approach.

5. In the *Status Bar* area, activate the Dynamic UCS option by clicking on the **UCSDETECT** option button as shown. (You can also hit [F6] once.)

6. Set the display option to the **Conceptual** visual style by clicking on the icon in the *Visual Styles* toolbar as shown.

7. Click on the **Cylinder** icon to activate the **Create Cylinder** command.

8. Move the cursor on top of any planar surface and notice the displayed dashed edges signifying the alignment of the *XY plane* of the temporary UCS to the surface.

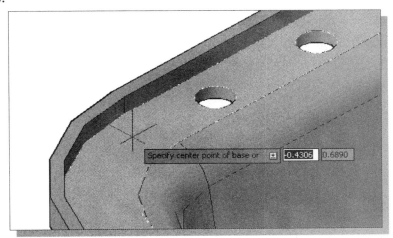

9. Pick an arbitrary location on the surface to use as the center point of the cylinder. Note the display of the alignment of the temporary UCS.

10. Enter **0.375** as the radius of the cylinder as shown.

11. Move the cursor upward and observe the preview of an extrusion as shown. (Note that moving the cursor in the opposite direction will create an extrusion in the opposite direction.)

12. Enter **1** as the height of the cylinder as shown.

• Note that we have successfully placed a cylinder on an existing surface. We can now move the cylinder to any desired location and join the cylinder to the main body. The Dynamic UCS approach reduced the tedious work of orienting the UCS prior to creating the necessary solid feature. In the next chapter, we will examine the use of Dynamic UCS as a powerful design tool.

Review Questions:

1. Describe the method used in the tutorial to create *Draft Angle* features in AutoCAD.

2. List and describe the differences between *Cut with a Pattern* and *Cut Each One Individually*.

3. Which command is used to create 3D rounded corners in AutoCAD?

4. What elements are required to define a *Rectangular Array* in AutoCAD?

5. How do we create a thin-walled part in AutoCAD? What elements are required to perform the operation?

6. Identify the following commands:

    (a)

    (b)

    (c)

    (d)

Exercises:

1. Dimensions are in inches.

2. Dimensions are in millimeters. (Note the two R40 arcs at the base share the same center.)

3. Dimensions are in inches.

Rounds & Fillets: R.125

4. Dimensions are in inches.

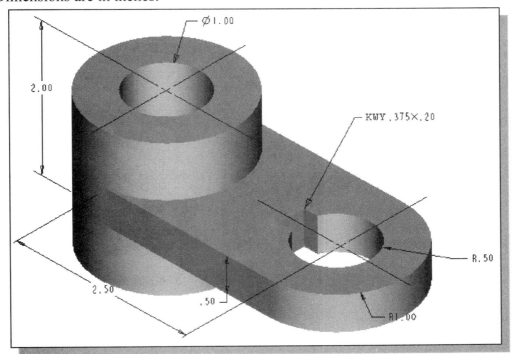

5.   Dimensions are in inches.

Chapter 11
Conceptual Design Tools & Techniques

Learning Objectives

- ◆ **Use the Conceptual Modeling Construction Tools**
- ◆ **Use the Dynamic UCS Option**
- ◆ **Use the Press/Pull Command**
- ◆ **Create Rectangular Patterns**
- ◆ **Use the Shell Command**
- ◆ **Use the Copy Faces Command**

Introduction

Engineering design is the ability to create and transform ideas and concepts into a product definition that meets the desired objective. The general procedure for the design of a new product, or improving an existing product, involves the following six stages:

1. **Develop and identify the desired objectives.**
2. **Conceptual design stage – Concepts and Ideas of possible solutions.**
3. **Computer Modeling and Engineering analysis of components.**
4. **Prototypes and testing.**
5. **Refine and finalize the design.**
6. **Working drawings of the finalized design.**

It is during the **conceptual design** stage when the first drawings, known as **conceptual drawings**, are usually created. The conceptual drawings are typically done in the form of freehand sketches showing the original ideas and concepts of possible solutions to the set objectives. From these conceptual drawings, engineering analyses are performed to improve and confirm the suitability of the proposed design. Working from the sketches and the results of the analyses, the design department then creates prototypes or performs computer simulations to further refine the design. Once the design is finalized, a set of detailed drawings of the proposed design are created.

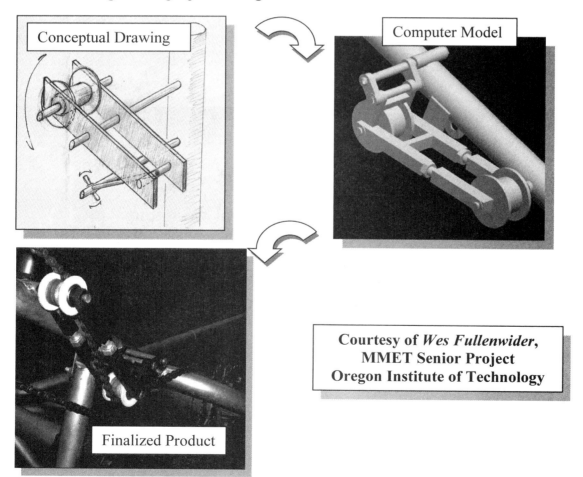

Conceptual Drawing

Computer Model

Finalized Product

Courtesy of *Wes Fullenwider*,
MMET Senior Project
Oregon Institute of Technology

During the **conceptual design** stage of the design process, the main emphasis is typically placed on the conceptualization of problems and solutions. Also, very little emphasis is placed on the finer details of the design during the conceptual design stage; only a few rough estimates of the actual sizes are considered.

The initial conceptual drawings and sketches represent the idea or essence of what the designer is trying to communicate. Getting the conceptual design correct at the beginning avoids the risk of costly redesign further down the line. Think about how expensive it would be to add a second bathroom once all the plumbing has been done.

One of the main enhancements of AutoCAD in recent years was the introduction of the 3D conceptual modeling tools, which allow the users to very quickly create 3D conceptual models. With the 3D conceptual computer models, the ideas and concepts of a design can be further examined and options explored. The introduction of the 3D conceptual modeling tools has made AutoCAD not just a drafting tool, but a very powerful design tool.

In this chapter, we will use a relatively simple design to illustrate the conceptual modeling tools that are available in AutoCAD 2017.

A *Bird House* Design

In this tutorial, we will create a 3D conceptual model of a *Bird House* design, based on the rough sketches shown below. Note that detailed dimensions are not of great concern during the conceptual design phase; only rough sizes are noted. This approach is also known as the **shape before size** design philosophy, where the primary concern is the shapes and forms of the design.

Approximate size: 30″ x 30″ x 25″

Starting Up AutoCAD 2017

1. Select the **AutoCAD 2017** option on the *Program* menu or select the **AutoCAD 2017** icon on the *Desktop*.

2. In the *Startup* window, select **Start from Scratch**, as shown in the figure below.

3. In the *Default Settings* section, pick **Imperial (feet and inches)** as the drawing units.

4. Pick **OK** in the *Startup* dialog box to accept the selected settings.

Layers Setup

1. In the *Menu Bar,* select **[Tools]** → **[Toolbars]** → **[AutoCAD]** → **[Layers]**.

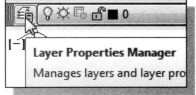

2. Click **Layers Properties Manager** in the *Layers* toolbar.

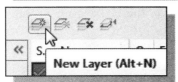

3. Click on the **New** button to create new layers.

4. Create **two new layers** with the following settings:

Layer	Color	Linetype	Lineweight
Base	Cyan	Continuous	Default
Roof	Blue	Continuous	Default

5. Highlight the layer **Base** in the list of layers.

6. Click on the **Current** button to set layer **Base** as the *Current Layer*.

7. Click on the **Close** button to accept the settings and exit the *Layer Properties Manager* dialog box.

8. In the *Status Bar* area, reset the options and turn *ON* the *Polar Tracking*, *Object Snap*, *Object Snap Tracking*, and *Dynamic Input* options.

The Base Plate

1. Move the cursor to the *View* control list and click on the **SE Isometric** view icon as shown.

2. In the *Modeling* toolbar, click on the **Box** icon. In the command prompt area, the message "*Specify corner of box or [Center] <0,0,0>:*" is displayed.

3. Place the first corner at the **origin** of the world coordinate system.

4. In the command prompt area, the message "*Specify corner or [Cube/Length]:*" is displayed. Enter **@30,30** [**ENTER**].

5. For the height of the box, enter **0.5** [**ENTER**].

6. In the *Navigation* toolbar, select the **Zoom All** command to adjust the display.

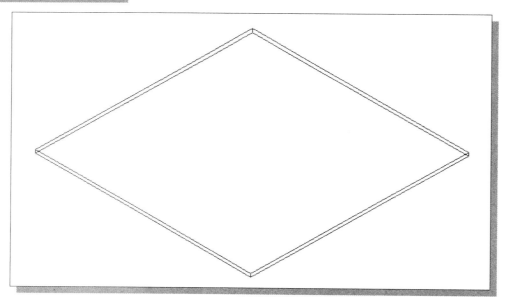

Create the Compartments for the 1st Floor

• In AutoCAD, the **Dynamic UCS** option can be used to quickly align UCS to existing surfaces. The dynamic UCS can be used to create objects on a planar face of a 3D solid without manually changing the UCS orientation.

1. Activate the *Dynamic UCS* option by clicking on the **associated** icon in the *Status Bar* as shown. (Use the **Customization** button to switch **on** the display.)

2. Select the **Rectangle** icon in the *Draw* toolbar. In the *command prompt area*, the message "*Specify first corner point or [Chamfer/Elevation/Fillet/Thickness/Width]:*" is displayed.

3. Move the cursor on the top plan of the 3D base and notice the dynamic UCS option automatically aligns the UCS to the top plane as shown.

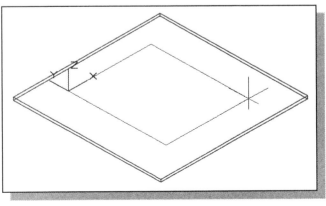

4. On your own, create a rectangle that is roughly ⅔ the size of the base as shown.

5. On your own, repeat the above steps and create four additional rectangles as shown in the figure below. Do not be overly concerned with the actual sizes and dimensions of the sketch; the main goal is "fast and loose" for conceptual models.

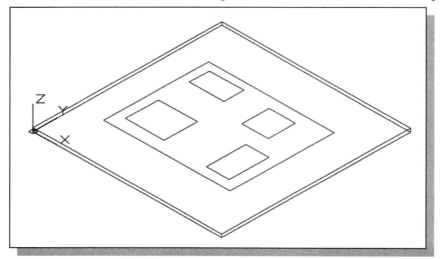

Create a Solid Feature Using the Press/Pull Command

- The **Press/Pull** command allows us to press or pull bounded areas. The bounded area must be bounded by coplanar lines or edges. This command can be activated through the icon panel or by pressing and holding [**CTRL + ALT**], and then picking the area.

1. Select **Press/Pull** in the *Modeling* toolbar as shown.

2. In the *command prompt area*, the message *"Click inside the bounded area to press or pull:"* is displayed. Move the cursor near the center of the 2D sketch and notice the dashed lines indicating the selected area.

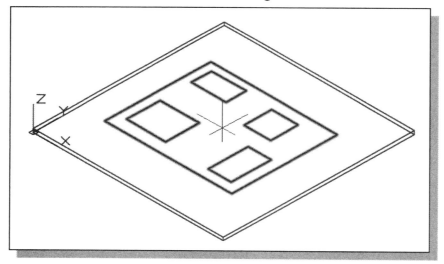

3. Inside the graphics window, use the **left-mouse-button** and **pull** the selection upward as shown.

4. Inside the graphics window, and **left-click** once to create the solid feature.

*   Note that the solid feature created with the Press/Pull command automatically joins the feature to the existing solid model. The Press/Pull command allows us the ability to create solids from 2D geometry. Note that this is a totally different approach than the **Region** command. This new approach was first introduced by the @Last Software Co. (now part of Google, Inc.) in their *SketchUp* software.

Using the Press/Pull Command as an Editing Tool

- The **Press/Pull** command can also be used as an editing tool. This command enables us to quickly resize any of the existing solid features.

1. Select **Press/Pull** in the *Modeling* toolbar as shown.

2. Move the cursor on top of the inside vertical wall of the lower-left compartment; note the highlighted lines indicating the currently **selectable** area.

3. Click once with the **left-mouse-button** to select the surface.

4. Move the cursor and notice the selected surface is being adjusted. Click with the left-mouse-button to accept the adjustment. Note that the individual surface can be moved and the model resized with the Press/Pull command.

Create another Cut Feature

1. In the *Draw* toolbar, click on the **Circle** icon to activate the circle command. In the command prompt area, the message "*Specify center point for circle or [3P/2P/Ttr]:*" is displayed.

2. Move the cursor on the front plane of the 3D base and notice the dynamic UCS option automatically aligns the UCS to the front plane as shown.

3. Pick a location to place the center point so that it is aligned to the center of the square opening.

4. Create a circle that is about half of the width of the square opening as shown in the figure below.

5. Inside the graphics window, select the circle by clicking once with the left-mouse-button. Notice that the 2D grip editing tool is also available for us to quickly adjust the size and location of the sketched 2D geometry.

6. Press the [**Esc**] key once to deselect any entities.

7. Select **Press/Pull** in the *Modeling* toolbar as shown. In the command prompt area, the message "*Click inside the bounded area to press or pull:*" is displayed.

8. Move the cursor near the center of the circle we just created and notice the highlighted lines indicating the selected area. (Hint: Use the **Zoom** functions to assist this operation.)

9. Inside the *graphics window*, press down the left-mouse-button and press the selection toward the right side and create the cut feature as shown.

Adjust the Compartments

1. Deactivate the *Object Snap* option by clicking on the **associated** icon in the *Status Bar* as shown.

2. On your own, use the **Free Orbit** option to view the current 3D solid model.

3. Select **Press/Pull** in the *Modeling* toolbar as shown. In the command prompt area, the message "*Click inside the bounded area to press or pull:*" is displayed.

4. On your own, adjust the compartments so that we can add additional compartments in between the existing ones, as shown in the figure below.

- The **Press/Pull** command enables us to perform fast and loose adjustments of existing surfaces, which conforms to the basic concept of conceptual design.

Add Additional Compartments

1. Select the **Rectangle** icon in the *Draw* toolbar. In the command prompt area, the message "*Specify first corner point or [Chamfer/Elevation/Fillet/Thickness/ Width]:*" is displayed.

2. Move the cursor on the top plane of the 3D base and notice the dynamic UCS option automatically aligns the UCS to the top plane.

3. On your own, create the four additional rectangles as shown in the figure below.

4. On your own, create the additional compartments using the **Press/Pull** command.

Create the Doors

1. Click on the **Circle** icon to activate the **Circle** command. In the command prompt area, the message "*Specify center point for circle or [3P/2P/Ttr]:*" is displayed.

2. Move the cursor on the front plan of the 3D base and notice the dynamic UCS option automatically aligns the UCS to the front plan as shown.

3. On your own, create the additional circles as shown in the figure below.

4. On your own, use the **Press/Pull** command and create the doors as shown in the figure below.

Create the 2nd Floor

- We will next create the 2nd floor of the bird house; we will do this by simply making a copy of the 1st floor model.

1. Choose **Copy** in the *Modify* toolbar. The message "*Select Objects:*" is displayed in the command prompt area.

2. Pick any surface of the 3D solid. Note the entire solid is selected.

3. Inside the *graphics window*, **right-click** to accept the selection and proceed with the Copy command.

4. On your own, drag and drop with the left-mouse-button to create a copy as shown.

5. Choose **3D Rotate** in the *3D Modeling and Editing* toolbar. The message "*Select Objects:*" is displayed in the *command prompt area.*

6. Pick any surface of the copy we just created. Note that we currently have two separate solid objects.

7. Inside the *graphics window*, **right-click** to accept the selection and proceed with the 3D Rotate command.

8. Pick a point near the center of the solid model.

9. Select the **horizontal ring** that is associated with the **Z** rotation axis as shown.

10. We will rotate the model 90 degrees about the Z-axis. Enter **90** as the rotation angle as shown.

11. The 2nd floor is now rotated 90 degrees; note that all of the AutoCAD solid modeling tools are also available for conceptual modeling.

Reposition the 2nd Floor

1. Click on the **Move** icon in the *Modify* toolbar. The message "*Select Objects:*" is displayed in the command prompt area.

2. Pick any surface of the 2nd floor model we just rotated.

3. Inside the *graphics window*, **right-click** to accept the selection and proceed with the Move command.

4. On your own, switch *ON* the **Object Snap Tracking** and the **Object Snap** options as shown in the figure below.

5. Select the lower left corner of the 2nd floor model as the **base point**, as shown in the figure.

6. Align the new location to the intersection of the lower and upper left corners of the 1st floor model as shown in the figure below. (Hint: Pause at the two reference corners and observe the dashed lines showing alignments.)

Modeling the Roof Section with the Press/Pull Command

1. Select the **Rectangle** icon in the *Draw* toolbar. In the command prompt area, the message *"Specify first corner point or [Chamfer/Elevation/Fillet/Thickness/Width]:"* is displayed.

2. Place the first corner point of the rectangle to the right side of the current 3D model.

3. We will create a rectangle that is the same size as the base of the model. Enter **@30,30** [ENTER].

4. Pick the **Press/Pull** icon in the *Solid* editing toolbar as shown in the figure.

5. Pick a location inside the rectangle we just created.

6. Move the cursor upward and enter **.5** as the height value as shown in the figure below.

7. Select the **Line** icon in the *Draw* toolbar. In the command prompt area, the message "*_line Specify first point:*" is displayed.

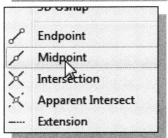

8. Inside the graphics window, hold down the [**SHIFT**] key and **right-click** once to bring up the *Object Snap* shortcut menu.

9. Select the **Midpoint** option in the pop-up window.

10. Place the first endpoint by snapping to the midpoint of the front top edge of the new model as shown.

11. Complete the line by making it perpendicular to the first selected edge and **extended beyond** the top of the rectangular block as shown.

Use the Imprint Command

- In AutoCAD, the appearance of a surface on a 3-D solid can be adjusted by imprinting the surface with an object that intersects with it. Imprinting combines the object with the surface, creating a new edge.

1. In the *Solid Editing toolbar*, click on the **Imprint** icon. In the command prompt area, the message *"Select a 3D Object:"* is displayed.

2. Select the **rectangular block** as the solid object to be adjusted.

3. In the *command prompt area*, the message *"Select an object to imprint:"* is displayed. Select the **line** we just created.

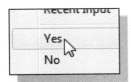

4. In the *command prompt area*, the message *"Delete the source object [Yes/No]:"* is displayed. Click once with the **right-click** to bring up the option menu and select **Yes** as shown.

5. In the *command prompt area*, the message *"Select an object to imprint:"* is displayed. Click once with the **right-mouse-button** to **end** the Imprint command.

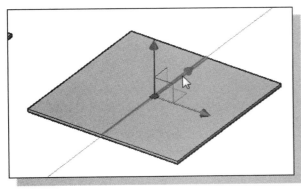

6. Hold down the [**CTRL**] key and move the cursor on top of the imprinted line we just created. Note that the two surfaces are also selectable; move the cursor around to cycle through the possible selections. Select the **line** when it is highlighted as shown.

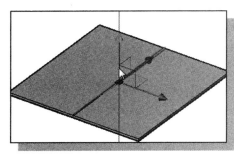

7. Move the cursor on top of the **vertical axis** near the center.

8. Drag the cursor **upward** to pull the center edge upward and adjust the rectangular shape of the solid model into a triangular shape as shown.

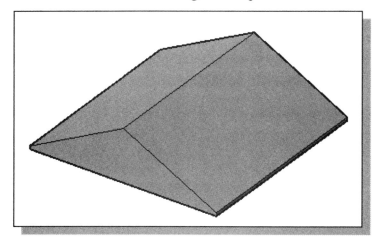

9. On your own, create a triangle aligned to the triangular surface of the roof as shown in the figure.

10. Pick the **Press/Pull** icon in the *Solid* editing toolbar as shown in the figure.

11. Pick a location inside the triangle we just created.

12. On your own, create a cut feature on the roof section as shown in the figure on the next page.

13. On your own, create a circular cut feature on the roof section as shown in the figure.

14. On your own, repeat the above steps to create similar features on the back side of the roof.

15. On your own, position the roof section on top of the 2nd floor model to complete the conceptual model of the bird house design as shown.

Review Questions:

1. Describe the general stages involved in an engineering design procedure.

2. What is the purpose of creating a *Conceptual Model*?

3. What are the main differences between a conceptual drawing and a detail drawing?

4. Which command can be used to quickly resize a 3D model in AutoCAD?

5. How do we alter an existing surface in AutoCAD? What elements are required to perform the operation?

6. Identify the following commands:

    (a)

    (b)

    (c)

    (d)

Exercises:

Create conceptual sketches and conceptual models of the following design projects:

1. **A better mousetrap.**

2. **A walking robot with four legs.**

3. **A rocket launcher.**

4. **A vehicle powered by birthday candles.**

5. **A hand-launched glider aircraft.**

6. **A Catapult for water balloons.**

7. **A vehicle to carry an egg safely down an inclined surface into a wall.**

8. **A vehicle to be powered solely by a hamster.**

9. **A rubber band powered all-terrain vehicle.**

Leveling Assembly (Create a set of detail and assembly drawings. All dimensions are in mm.)

(a) **Base Plate**

(b) **Sliding Block** (Rounds & Fillets: R3)

(c) Lifting Block (Rounds & Fillets: R3)

(d) **Adjusting Screw** (M10 X 1.5)

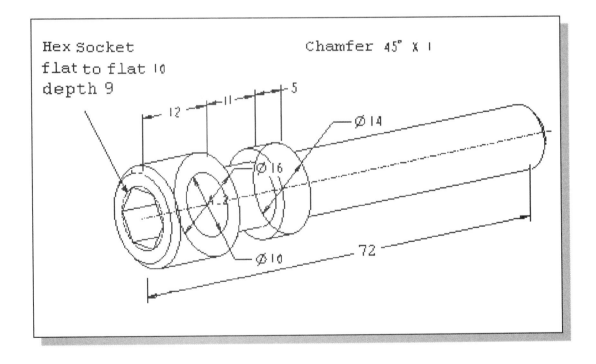

Hex Socket
flat to flat 10
depth 9

Chamfer 45° X 1

Ø 14

Ø 16

12   11   5

Ø 10

72

Notes:

Chapter 12
Introduction to Photorealistic Rendering

Learning Objectives

♦ **Use the Basic Rendering Tools**
♦ **Use the Lighting Simulation Options**
♦ **Add Individual Lights to the Scene**
♦ **Create and Modify Materials**
♦ **Use the Sun & Sky Background Command**

Introduction

In this chapter, we will examine the tools available in AutoCAD to perform photorealistic rendering. The purpose of photorealistic rendering is to help the engineers/designers communicate their design concepts. In AutoCAD we can use the different rendering options to create 2D photorealistic images based on the constructed 3D models and scenes. Using **Render**, it is possible to add realistic materials and lighting to get the most realistic view of the design. AutoCAD will generate photorealistic images by applying the selected materials to the models, adding effects of environmental settings, such as background images, or the effects of fog and shadows can be included in the rendering.

It is important to note that rendering can be a very time-consuming task. For example, if multiple light sources are included in the setup, and each of them casts shadows, a considerable amount of computing power will be required. One can also spend a lot of time adjusting materials, camera and lighting positions/angles. With AutoCAD 2017 it is now possible to preview many aspects of the final image before actually performing the rendering. And it is also feasible to do initial renderings at lower quality settings or render just a portion of the final image to check the effects before creating a final high-resolution rendering.

The process of creating a computerized photorealistic rendering usually involves the five steps below:
1. **Create the 3D models of the design.**
2. **Create and adjust the environmental settings.**
3. **Attach materials to the models.**
4. **Create and place lights.**
5. **Render the photorealistic image.**

Once the CAD objects are drawn, you have to decide which materials to use. AutoCAD comes with a basic materials library that you can use to apply to the objects. Applying the materials is a relatively easy process, but getting them to look exactly the way we want can be a skill in itself. There are three types of lights in AutoCAD: **Point**, **Spotlight** and **Distant**. We will examine how each one is created and adjusted.

Startup AutoCAD 2017 and Retrieve the Pulley Design

1. Select the **AutoCAD 2017** option on the *Program* menu or select the **AutoCAD 2017** icon on the *Desktop*.

2. In the *Startup* window, select **Open a Drawing**, as shown in the figure below.

3. Select **Pulley.dwg** as the drawing to be opened. Use the **Browse** button to search for the file if it is not displayed in the files list.

4. Pick **OK** in the *Startup* dialog box to accept the selected drawing.

Environment Setup

1. In the *View* toolbar, select **Realistic** as the *Visual Styles* type as shown.

   ➢ The **Realistic** *Visual Style* provides a relatively good representation of the constructed model.

2. Set the **Object_lines** layer as the current *Layer* as shown.

3. Set the *View* display to **Top** as shown.

4. Click on the **Rectangle** button to activate the Rectangle command.

   ➢ We will create a 2D region representing the floor of the environment.

5. On your own, create a rectangle so that the *Pulley* sits roughly near the center of the floor as shown.

6. Activate the **Region** command by clicking on the button in the *Draw* toolbar as shown.

7. Select the **rectangle** we just created.

8. Inside the *graphics area*, **right-click** once to accept the selection.

9. Set the *View* display to **SE Isometric** as shown.

10. Select the rectangular **region** we just created.

11. Move the cursor on top of the front corner of the rectangle as shown.

➢ The grip editing options, available in AutoCAD, allow us to quickly perform many editing options to the selected geometry.

12. Select the **vertical axis** to restrict the movement in the selected direction.

13. On your own, move the selected rectangular region downward so that the entire *Pulley* design is above the floor.

14. Hit the **[Esc]** key once to de-select the rectangular region.

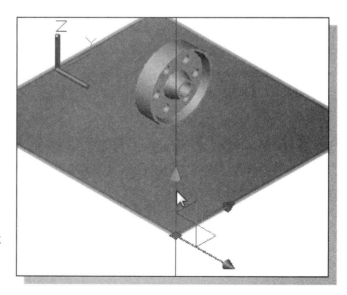

Use the Render Command

➢ To illustrate the effects of the different rendering options, we will first execute the **Render** command using the default setups and without applying any materials or lights.

1. Click on the **Visualize** tab in the *Ribbon* toolbar area to display the render related toolbars as shown.

2. In the *Render* toolbar, click on the **Render** icon. Note that we are using the default settings.

➢ A separate *Render* window appears on the screen.

➢ The default lighting system is a fast and simple system where the rendered image is very rough and does not have any realistic feel to it.

3. Hit the **[Esc]** key once to close the *Render* window.

Available Lighting Simulation Modes in AutoCAD

- Three types of lighting simulations are available in AutoCAD; each offers their own advantages and disadvantages.

Default Lighting Simulation Mode

When there are no lights in a scene, the scene is shaded with *Default Lighting*. *Default Lighting* mode is derived from two distant sources that follow the viewpoint as the user moves around the model. All faces in the model are illuminated so that they are visually discernible.

When custom lights or sunlight are added into the scene, the *Default Lighting* can be disabled. The *Default Lighting* mode is a fast and simple lighting simulation that does not require much computing power to render.

Standard Lighting Simulation Mode

To give the scene a more realistic appearance, the *Standard Lighting* simulation can be used. Individual lights can be added and properties adjusted, and the lighting system enhances the clarity and three-dimensionality of a scene. The user can create **point lights**, **spotlights**, and **distant lights** to achieve the desired effects. Added lights can be moved or rotated with grip editing tools; they can be turned *ON* and *OFF*, and properties can be changed. The effects of changes are visible in the viewport in real time.

Spotlights and *point lights* are each represented by a different light glyph (a symbol in the drawing showing the location of the light). Distant lights and the sun are not represented by glyphs in the drawing because they do not have a discrete position and affect the entire scene. The light glyphs can be used to control the position and properties of the related lights.

Photometric Lighting Simulation Mode

For more precise control over lighting, the *Photometric Light* simulation mode can be used to illuminate the scene. *Photometric Lighting* simulation mode uses ***photometric*** (light energy) values that define lights more accurately as they would be in the real world. Lights with various distribution and color characteristics can be created, and specific photometric files available from lighting manufacturers can be imported into the scene.

Photometric Lighting simulation mode can use manufacturers' ***IES*** standard file format. By using manufacturers' lighting data, commercially available lighting can be simulated in the model. This provides the most realistic lighting results. We can experiment with different fixtures, and by varying the light intensity and color temperature, we can design a lighting system mode that produces the desirable results. Note that it may require a considerable amount of computing power with this simulation mode.

Use the Materials Options

- In AutoCAD, the **Dynamic UCS** option can be used to quickly align the UCS to existing surfaces. The *Dynamic UCS* can be used to create objects on a planar face of a 3D solid without manually changing the UCS orientation.

1. Select the **Materials Browser** icon in the *Materials* toolbar to open the AutoCAD *Materials Browser*.

➤ In the *Materials Browser* window, two libraries are available as default. The **Autodesk Library** contains the pre-defined materials that are commonly used for Architectural and Mechanical Engineering designs. The second library available is **Favorites**, which is currently empty; this is for user-defined materials.

2. Select the **Autodesk Library** by clicking on the icon if necessary.

3. On your own, use the scrollbar and examine the different materials available.

4. Click on the **add material to document** button on **1in Square-Ivory** in the materials list. Note that the selected material is now listed in the *Document Materials* section near the top of the *Materials Browser* window.

5. *Drag and drop* the **1in Square-Ivory** material, the icon shown in the *Document Materials* section, on top of the floor region as shown.

6. On your own, repeat the above steps and apply the **Beechwood-Galliano** material to the *Pulley* design.

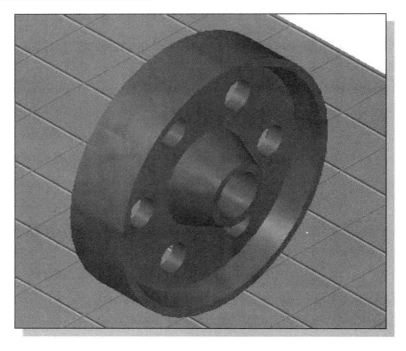

Activate the Sun & Sky Background Option

1. Type **Background** in the *command prompt area* as shown.

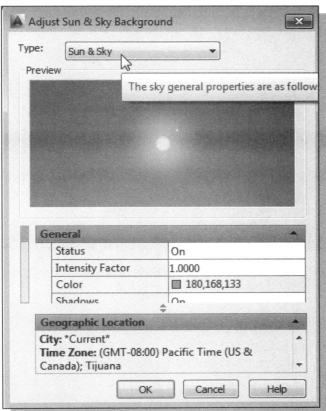

2. In the ***Adjust Sun & Sky Background*** window, set the background *Type* to **Sun & Sky**.

➢ Note that the *Sun & Sky* background can be used to simulate a 3D outdoor environment. The geographic location and time are initially set based on the user's computer settings.

3. Click **OK** to accept the settings.

➢ Notice the ***Sun and Sky Background*** options become activated in the *Ribbon* toolbar area.

4. In the *Render* toolbar, click on the **Render** icon. Note that we are using the default settings.

➢ The ***Render*** window appears on the screen, and it will take a bit longer to generate the rendered image.

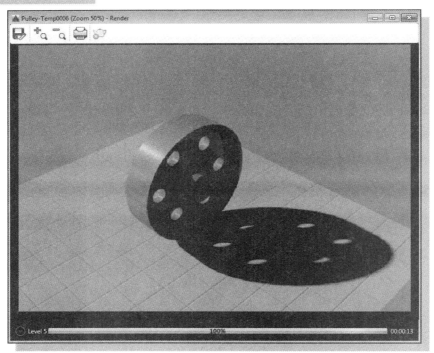

5. On your own, use the mouse-wheel to Zoom In/Out. Hit the [**Esc**] key once to close the *Render* window.

6. Click on the small **down arrow** displayed in the *Sun & Location* toolbar to bring up the ***Sun Properties*** dialog box.

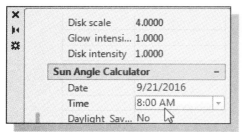

7. Set the *Time* to earlier in the morning, such as **8:00 AM**, by selecting the time list as shown.

8. Click **Close** to exit the *Sun Properties* dialog box.

9. In the *Render* toolbar, set the *Render resolution* option to **High** as shown.

10. In the *Render* toolbar, click on the **Render** icon to start the Render command.

11. Hit the [**Esc**] key once to close the *Render* window.

12. On your own, adjust the ***Time*** and ***Date*** settings to see the different effects.

➢   Setting the ***Time*** to earlier in the day, or later in the afternoon, will produce longer shadows than at midday.

Add Additional Walls

1. Click on the **Home** tab in the *Ribbon* toolbar area as shown.

2. Activate the **Copy** command by clicking on the corresponding icon as shown.

3. Select the **floor** as the object to be copied.

4. Click once with the **right-mouse-button** to accept the selection.

5. Select the **left corner** of the rectangular region as a reference point.

6. Select the **same location** again. We have created a copy at the same location of the original rectangular region.

7. **Right-click** once to bring up the option list.

8. Select **Exit** to end the Copy command.

9. Activate the **3D Rotate** command by clicking on the corresponding icon as shown.

10. Select one copy of the overlapping rectangular regions.

11. Click once with the **right-mouse-button** to accept the selection.

12. Select the **left corner** as the base point for the rotation operation.

13. Select the **green circle** to set the rotation axis.

14. Enter **90** as the rotation angle as shown.

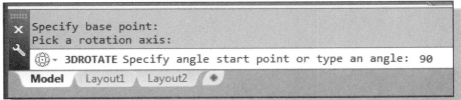

15. On your own, repeat the above steps and create the other side wall.

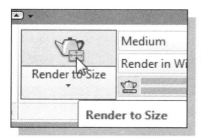

16. In the *Render* toolbar, click on the **Render** icon to start the Render command.

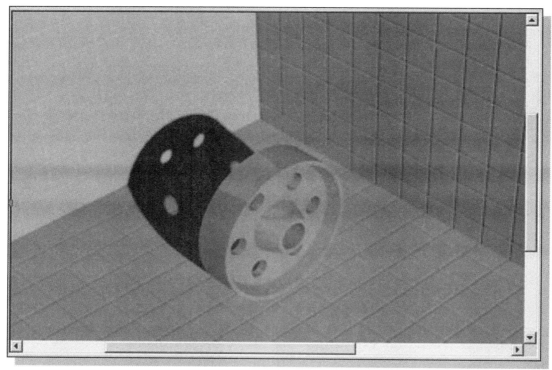

17. Hit the [**Esc**] key once to close the *Render* window.

18. Click on the **Sun Status** icon to toggle *OFF* the lighting effects of the sun.

➤ Note that the **Sky Background** can also be turned *OFF* in the toolbar area as shown.

Create a Point Light

- A point light radiates light in all directions from its location. A point light does not target an object. Use point lights for general lighting effects. To use the individual lights for more realistic rendering, the *Default Lighting* mode needs to be switched *OFF*.

1. In the *Lights* toolbar, click on the **Default Lighting** icon to turn it *OFF*. Note that one of the *Photometric Lighting* modes will be switched *ON* when the *Default Lighting* is turned *OFF*.

2. In the *Lights* toolbar, click on the **Create Point Light** icon to activate the command.

3. Set the display option to **Top** view by clicking on the top face of the ViewCube as shown.

4. Place the point light in front of the *Pulley* design and near the right side wall as shown.

5. Click once with the **right-mouse-button** to bring up the option list and select **Enter** to create the point light.

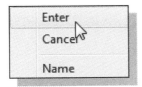

6. On your own, reset the display to **SE Isometric**.

7. In the *Render* toolbar, click on the **Render** icon to start the Render command.

8. On your own, reposition the point light higher by using the grip editing options.

9. On your own, use the **Render** command to examine the effects of repositioning the point light.

Changing the Applied Materials

1. Select the **Materials Browser** icon in the *Materials* toolbar to open the AutoCAD *Materials Browser*.

2. Add the **Flaked Reflective – Beige** material to the *Document Materials* list as shown.

3. Drag and drop the **Flaked Reflective** material on top of the **Pulley** design as the new material.

4. Add the **Coarse Textured – Light Orange** material to the *Document Materials* list as shown.

5. Drag and drop the **Coarse Textured** material on top of the **walls** as the new material.

6. Any material listed in the *Document Materials* list can also be removed by using the option list as shown.

7. On your own, use the **Render** command to examine the effects of the newly applied materials.

Create a Spotlight

- A spotlight distribution casts a focused beam of light like a flashlight, a follow spot in a theater, or a headlight.

1. In the *Lights* toolbar, click on the **Create Spotlight** icon to activate the command.

2. Set the display option to **Top** view by clicking on the top face of the ViewCube as shown.

3. Place the spotlight close to the *Pulley* design as shown.

4. Switch to the **SE Isometric** view by clicking on the corresponding corner of the ViewCube as shown.

5. Set the spotlight to point downward as shown.

6. Use the **right-mouse-button** to bring up the option list and select **Enter** to create the spotlight.

7. On your own, experiment with the **grip-editing tools** and adjust the spotlight so that it is above the *Pulley* design. (Hint: Click at the center of the triad to reposition the spotlight.)

- The intensity of the lights can be set through **Right-Click - Properties** option.

8. On your own, set the *Render* resolution to **Medium**.

9. In the *Render* toolbar, click on the **Render** icon to start the Render command.

- Note that the rendering requires many more calculations as the settings, such as additional materials and lights, become more complex.

Removing a Light

- Lights can be removed just as easily as they can be added to the scene.

1. Click on the **point light** icon to pre-select it in the graphics area.

2. Hit the [**Delete**] key once to remove the selected point light.

3. On your own, use the **Render** command and examine the effects without the point light.

Create a Distant Light

- A *distant light* emits uniform parallel light rays in one direction only. A *From* point and a *To* point are required to define the direction of the light. The intensity of a distant light does not diminish over distance; it is as bright at each face it strikes as it is at the source. Distant lights are useful for lighting objects or for lighting a backdrop uniformly. The lighting of the *Sun & Sky Background* option is an example of the effects of a *distant light*.

1. In the *Lights* toolbar, switch to using the **Generic lighting** simulation mode. Note that the *Generic lighting* simulation mode is also known as the AutoCAD *Standard Lighting* mode.

- The *Standard Lighting* simulation can be used to give the scene a more realistic appearance. Individual lights can be added and properties adjusted. The user can create **point lights**, **spotlights**, and **distant lights** to achieve the desired effects. The effects of changes are visible in the viewport in real time.

2. In the *Lights* toolbar, click on the **Distant Light** icon to activate the command.

3. Click **Allow** to add the additional distance light to the current system.

4. Set the display option to **SE Isometric** view by clicking on the corresponding corner of the ViewCube as shown.

5. In the *Status Bar* area, switch **ON** the *Object Snap* and *Object Snap Tracking* modes as shown.

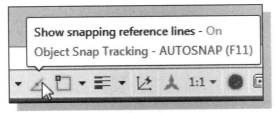

- Note that *distant lights* are not represented by glyphs in the drawing because they do not have a discrete position and affect the entire scene. We will use the *Object Snap* options to position the distant light.

6. Move the cursor to the upper right corner of the right vertical wall to activate the *Object Snap Tracking* option.

7. Also move the cursor to the front corner of the floor to activate the *Object Snap Tracking* option.

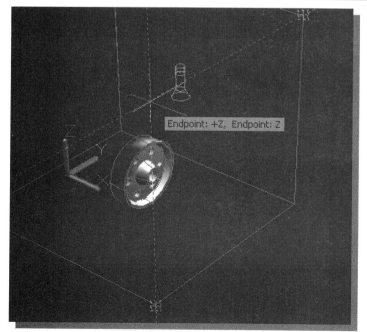

8. Place the distant light right at the intersection of the *Object Tracking Options* as shown.

•   A *From* point and a *To* point are required to define the direction of the light. We have identified the *From* point.

9. Snap to the right endpoint of the centerline, or the center point of the *Pulley* design, as shown.

10. Click once with the **right-mouse-button** to bring up the option list and select **Exit** to create the distant light.

11. On your own, use the **Render** command and examine the effects with the added distant light.

Create New Materials

1. Select the **Materials Browser** icon in the *Materials* toolbar to open the AutoCAD *Materials Browser*.

2. Click on the **Create Material** icon at the bottom of the *Materials Browser* dialog box as shown.

3. Select **Generic Material** as the category for the new material.

•   The displayed swatch and the quality of the preview can be adjusted by clicking on the down arrow as shown.

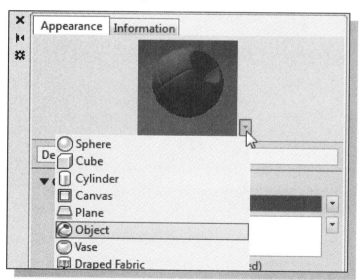

4. Enter **Solid Red** as the name of the new material.

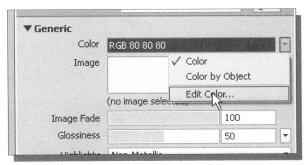

5. Click on the **down arrow** next to the *Color* box to display the option list.

6. Select **Edit Color** in the list as shown.

7. Set the *Color* to **250,0,0** for the RGB elements as shown.

8. Click **OK** to accept the settings.

9. Click on the check box next to the ***Reflectivity*** option and set the *Direct* and *Oblique Reflectivity* values to **30** as shown. Note that *0* means *no reflections* and *100* means *maximum reflections*.

10. Click **Close** to accept the settings and exit the *Material Editor*.

11. Note the newly created material is listed in the *Document Materials* list as shown.

12. Drag and drop the **Solid Red** material on the *Pulley* design to assign the new material.

13. On your own, use the **Render** command and examine the effects with the added material.

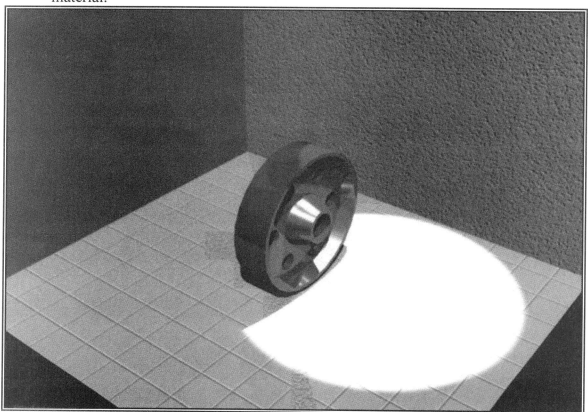

14. Hit the **[Esc]** key once to close the *Render* window.

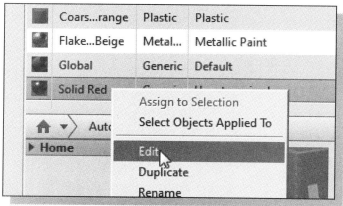

15. **Right-click** on the **Solid Red** icon and select **Edit** in the option list as shown.

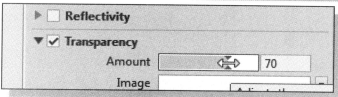

16. On your own, experiment with the different settings available.

Save the Rendered Images

- Two options are available to save the rendered images.

1. Choose **File → Save** in the *Render Window* toolbar.

2. In the *Render Output File* dialog box, choose the desired output image format, such as **BMP**, **JPEG**.

3. Enter a file name in the *File name* box as shown.

4. Click **Save** to save the image.

5. Inside the graphics window, **right-click** on any of the rendered images to bring up the option list.

6. Select **Save** to save the selected image to disk.

Conclusion

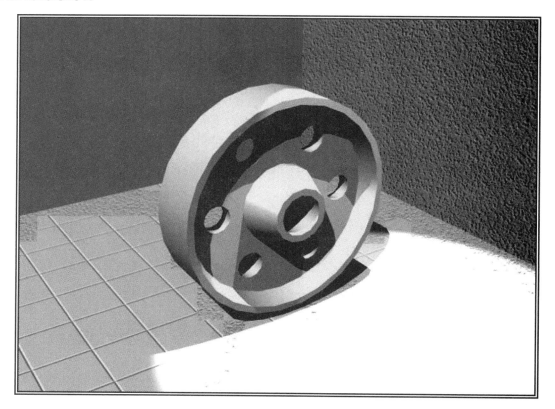

Design includes all activities involved from the original concept to the finished product. Design is the process by which products are created and modified. For many years designers sought ways to describe and analyze three-dimensional designs without building physical models. With the advancements in computer technology, the creation of solid models on computers offers a wide range of benefits. Solid models are easier to interpret and can be easily altered. Solid models can also be analyzed using finite element analysis software, and simulations of real-life loads can be applied to the models and the results can be graphically displayed.

Throughout this text various modeling techniques have been presented. Mastering these techniques will enable you to create intelligent and flexible solid models. The goal is to make use of the tools provided by AutoCAD and to successfully create solid models of the design. In many instances, only a single approach to the modeling tasks was presented; you are encouraged to repeat all of the chapters and develop different ways of thinking in accomplishing the tasks. We have only scratched the surface of AutoCAD's functionality. The more time you spend using the system, the easier it will be to perform design and modeling tasks with AutoCAD.

Review Questions:

1. Describe the general procedure to create a photorealistic rendering in AutoCAD.

2. What are the different lighting simulation modes available in AutoCAD?

3. Which lighting simulation mode produces the most realistic rendering?

4. What are the three different types of lights we can create in AutoCAD? Provide a brief description for each type of light.

5. How do we create and alter a material in AutoCAD?

6. Identify the following commands:

   (a)

   (b)

   (c)

   (d)

Exercises:

1. Render the birdhouse created in Chapter 11 using the *Sun & Sky Background* option.

2. Render the *Guide-Block* design created in Chapter 6 using the *Spotlight* and *Distant light* options. (Hint: Adjust the intensity of the lights to create different effects.)

INDEX

A

Arcball, 3-16
Array, 3D, 9-16
Axonometric projection, 1-2

B

Binary Tree, 6-4
Block, solids, 6-7
Boolean Intersect, 6-3
Boolean Operations, 6-3
Boundary Representation (B-rep), 7-2
Box, Solid, 6-7
Box Method, 3-2
Break, 5-21
Buttons, Mouse, Intro-12

C

CAD, Intro-2
CAE, Intro-2
Canceling commands, Intro-12
Cartesian Coordinate System, 2-16
CIRCLE command, 3-19
Close dialog box, 2-19
Close window, 4-4
Coincident constraint, 1-33
Combine Parts, 9-14
Command prompt, Intro-8, Intro-10
Command line area, Intro-9
Computer Geometric Modeling, Intro-2
Conceptual design, 11-2
Conceptual Visual Style, 5-8
Constraints, Hide All, 1-34
Construction Line, 8-18
Constructive solid geometry, 6-2
Coordinate systems, 2-16
Coordinates, 2-9
Copy Faces, 10-8
Copy Object, 1-21, 3-20
Create Drawings, Intro-7
Create Material, 12-26
CSG, 6-3
Current UCS, 4-20
Cursor Coordinates Display, Intro-10

Customization icon, 1-7
Cylinder, Solid, 6-9

D

Dimetric projections, 1-2
Display Locked, 8-18
Distant Light, 12-23
Draft Angle, 10-10
Drafting Settings, 2-7, 4-8
Draw toolbar, 2-9
Drawing Layout, 8-4
Drawing Limits, 2-6
Drawing Views, Scale, 8-17
DUCS, 10-24, 11-7
DVIEW, 8-16

E

Edge, hidden, 5-16
Endpoint, snap, 2-13
Erase, 2-15
Esc, Intro-12
EXIT, Intro-14
Explode, 3-17
Extract faces, 10-8
Extend, 4-23
Extrude, 7-2, 7-15
Extrude, Draft Angle, 10-10

F

Face, 3D, 5-2, 5-10, 5-14
FILLET, 10-6
Fillet, 3D, 10-16, 10-17
Fix constraint, 1-32
Folder, create new, Intro-14
Format, pull-down, 2-5
Four Viewports, 4-14
Free Orbit, 3-16
From, Snap, 3-11
Front view, 4-23

G

Global space, 2-16

Graphics window, Intro-8, Intro-9
GRID Interval setup, 2-7
GRIP, editing, 4-23, 5-17, 10-23

H
Help, Intro-13
Help Line, Intro-8, Intro-13
Hide, 2-20
Hidden, 2D, 3D 5-8, 5-13

I
Imprint, 11-21
Inquiry, 7-17
INTERSECT, 4-9
Invisible Edge, 5-16
Isocircle, 1-14, 1-15
ISODRAFT, 1-5
ISOPLANE, 1-5
Isometric projections, 1-2
Isometric Views, 2-17

J
JOIN, 6-3

L
Layers Control toolbar, Intro-11
Layer, New, 1-6
Layer Properties Manager, 1-6, 2-21
Layout, 8-7
Layout tab, 8-4
Lighting Simulation, 12-8
Limits, 2-6
LINE command, 3-9
Line, Close, 7-9
Local Coordinate System (LCS), 2-16

M
Mass Properties, 7-17
Materials, 12-9
Meshes, 5-2, 5-5
Midpoint, Snap, 2-11
Mirror, 4-15, 7-14
Mirror 3D, 9-13
Model Space, 8-4
Model tab, 8-11

Model mode, 8-7, 8-11
Modeling toolbar, 6-7
Modify toolbar, 2-10
Mouse Buttons, Intro-12
Move, 6-17
Move UCS, 2-23
Multiview drawing, 8-2, 8-10

N
Named view, 4-20
New UCS, 4-18
New UCS, Face, 7-18

O
Object Properties toolbar, 2-23, 4-12, 4-17, 5-19, 7-8, 8-7
Object Snap, 1-11, 2-11
Object Snap settings, 4-8
Object Snap toolbar, 3-10
OFFSET, 2-9
On-Line Help, Intro-13
One Viewport, 4-17
Open a Drawing, 5-4, 5-18
Orbit, Free, 3-16

P
Page Setup, 8-4
Pan Realtime, 8-8
Paper Space, 8-4
Parametric toolbar, 1-32
Photometric, 12-8
Plan view, 4-20
Polar Angle settings, 4-8
Polar Tracking, 4-8
Polygonal Viewport, 8-13
Polyline, 2-9
Point light, 12-17
Press/Pull, 11-8
Primitive Solids, 6-3
Properties, 2-19
Pull-down menus, Intro-8

Q
Quadrant, Snap to, 3-21
Quick Select, 4-15

Quit, Intro-14

R

Realistic Visual Style, 5-8
RECTANGLE command, 2-25
RECTANGULAR Array, 10-19
Reference area setup, 2-6
Regen, 8-16
Region, 5-2, 7-10
Region, Subtract, 9-8
Render, 12-2
Repeat, 3-9
Revolve, 7-2, 9-12
Revolved Feature, 9-2
Revolved Surfaces, 5-3, 5-20
ROTATE, 7-6
Rotate Faces, 6-16
Rotate, 3D, 7-12
Rotate UCS, 2-27
Rounds, 3D, 10-16
Ruled Surfaces, 5-3, 5-20, 5-24

S

SAVE AS, 2-15
Scale Drawing Views, 8-17
Screen Layout, Intro-8
SE Isometric, 2-17
Selection window, 2-18
Settings, 4-8
Shade toolbar, 5-8
Shaded Solids, 6-14
Shape before size, 11-3
SHELL, 10-18
Show Startup dialog box, 3-4
Single Line Help, Intro-8
Snap from, 2-13
Snap Interval Setup, 2-7
Snap to Endpoint, 2-13
Snap to Midpoint, 1-22, 2-11
Snap to Quadrant, 3-21
Solid Editing, 10-8
Solid Modelers, Intro-4
Solid, 2D, 5-2
SOLPROF, 8-21
Spotlight, 12-20
Standard Scale property, 8-17

Start From Scratch, 3-5
Startup options, 3-4
Startup window, 3-5
Status Toolbar, Intro-10
SteeringWheels, 6-18
Stretch, 4-24
Subtract, 6-3, 6-12
Sun & Sky Background, 12-11
Surface Modelers, Intro-4
Surface Modeling commands, 5-20
Surfaces toolbars, 5-5
SW Isometric view, 4-24
Symmetrical Features, 9-2

T

Tabulated Surfaces, 5-3, 5-20, 5-23
Tangent constraint, 1-33
Taper Angle, 10-10
Thickness, 2-2, 2-19
Thickness option, Rectangle, 2-25
3 Point, UCS, 4-18, 5-5
3D Face, 5-10
3D Hidden, 2-20
3D Modeling, Intro-3
3D Rounds and Fillets, 10-16
3D view, 2-17
3D Wireframe, 3-2~3-4, 3-17, 5-8
Thin Shell, 10-18
Title Block, 8-6
Tools, pull-down, 2-7
Top view, 4-14
Trim, 2-14
Trimetric projections, 1-2
2½D solid modeling approach, 2-19
2D Extrusion method, 3-2
2D Drafting & Annotation, 2-4
2D Wireframe, 2-29

U

Undo, 2-14
Union, 6-10
Units Setup, 2-5
UCS, 2-2, 4-7, 5-5
UCS, 3 point, 4-18
UCS icon, 4-19
UCS II, 4-7

UCS Toolbar, 4-7
User Coordinate System (UCS), 2-2
User Coordinate System, 2-15

V
View, Hidden 3D, 2-20
View, named, 4-20
View, 3D Views, 3-7
View toolbar, 3-16
ViewCube, 5-12
Viewports, 4-14
Viewport Scale, 8-17
Visual Styles, 2-29, 5-8
Visualize, 12-7

W
Wireframe, 2D, 5-8
Wireframe, 3D, 3-2~3-4, 3-17, 5-8
Wireframe Modeler, Intro-3
Wizard, quick setup, 3-5
World Coordinate System, 2-18
World space, 2-15
World UCS, 5-9

X
X-Axis Rotate UCS, 2-27
XY-Plane, 3-7

Y
YZ-Plane, 2-16

Z
Zoom All, 2-7, 4-6
ZX-Plane, 2-16

About Us

SDC Publications specializes in creating exceptional books that are designed to seamlessly integrate into courses or help the self learner master new skills. Our commitment to meeting our customer's needs and keeping our books priced affordably are just some of the reasons our books are being used by nearly 1,200 colleges and universities across the United States and Canada.

SDC Publications is a family owned and operated company that has been creating quality books since 1985. All of our books are proudly printed in the United States.

Our technology books are updated for every new software release so you are always up to date with the newest technology. Many of our books come with video enhancements to aid students and instructor resources to aid instructors.

Take a look at all the books we have to offer you by visiting SDCpublications.com.

NEVER STOP LEARNING

Keep Going

Take the skills you learned in this book to the next level or learn something brand new. SDC Publications offers books covering a wide range of topics designed for users of all levels and experience. As you continue to improve your skills, SDC Publications will be there to provide you the tools you need to keep learning. Visit SDCpublications.com to see all our most current books.

Why SDC Publications?

- Regular and timely updates
- Priced affordably
- Designed for users of all levels
- Written by professionals and educators
- We offer a variety of learning approaches

TOPICS

3D Animation
BIM
CAD
CAM
Engineering
Engineering Graphics
FEA / CAE
Interior Design
Programming

SOFTWARE

Adams
ANSYS
AutoCAD
AutoCAD Architecture
AutoCAD Civil 3D
Autodesk 3ds Max
Autodesk Inventor
Autodesk Maya
Autodesk Revit
CATIA
Creo Parametric
Creo Simulate
Draftsight
LabVIEW
MATLAB
NX
OnShape
SketchUp
SOLIDWORKS
SOLIDWORKS Simulation